David Livingstone

Pocket BIOGRAPHIES

David Livingstone

C.S. NICHOLLS

SUTTON PUBLISHING

First published in 1998 by
Sutton Publishing Limited · Phoenix Mill
Thrupp · Stroud · Gloucestershire · GL5 2BU

British Library Cataloguing in Publication Data
A catalogue record for this book is available from the British
Library.

ISBN 0-7509-1591-9

ALAN SUTTON™ and SUTTON™ are the
trade marks of Sutton Publishing Limited

Typeset in 12/16 pt Perpetua.
Typesetting and origination by
Sutton Publishing Limited
Printed in Great Britain by
The Guernsey Press Company Limited
Guernsey, Channel Islands.

For

Caroline and Isabel

CONTENTS

CHRONOLOGY

1813	**19 March.** Livingstone born in Blantyre, Scotland
1823	Begins work in cotton mill
1836	Begins medical studies at Anderson College, Glasgow
1838	Trains at London Missionary Society seminary
1840	**20 November.** Ordained
1841	**15 March.** Arrives in South Africa
	31 July. Arrives at Kuruman mission station
1841–3	Three journeys northwards from Kuruman
1844	Sets up mission station at Mabotsa
1845	**2 January.** Marries Mary, Robert Moffat's daughter
1845	Sets up mission station at Chonwane. First child, Robert, born
1847	Abandons Chonwane and sets up mission station at Kolobeng. Second child, Agnes, born
1849	Third child, Thomas, born
	1 August. Reaches Lake Ngami
1850	Second journey to Lake Ngami. Fourth child, Elizabeth, born and dies six weeks later
1851	Journey to the Chobe and Zambezi rivers. Fifth child, (William) Oswell, born
1852	**23 April.** Sends his family home to Scotland

Chronology

1853	**23 May.** Reaches the Kololo settlement at Linyanti
1854	**May.** Reaches, overland, Luanda on west coast of Africa
1854–5	**September–August.** Travels from Luanda to Linyanti
1855–6	**November–May.** Linyanti–Zambezi river–Victoria Falls–Quelimane on east coast of Africa
1856	**July–December.** Sails from Mauritius to England via Red Sea
1857	Publishes *Missionary Travels and Researches in South Africa*
1858	**10 March.** Leaves England for South Africa
1858	Sixth child, Anna Mary, born
1859	Explores River Shire and reaches Lake Nyasa
1860	Travels up the Zambezi to Barotseland and returns to east coast
1862	**27 April.** Death of wife, Mary, at Shupanga on the Zambezi
1863	**July.** Expedition to Zambezi recalled by British government
1864	Takes river launch *Lady Nyassa* across Indian Ocean to Bombay
	23 July. Reaches England
1865	Publication of *Narrative of an Expedition to the Zambezi*
1866	**January.** Sails from Bombay to Zanzibar
	March. Begins expedition up Rovuma river

<table>
<tr><td>1866–8</td><td>Travels in interior around lakes Nyasa, Tanganyika, Mweru and Bangweulu</td></tr>
<tr><td>1869</td><td>Becomes ill and is carried into Ujiji
21 September. Reaches Bambarre</td></tr>
<tr><td>1870</td><td>**February–June.** Ill at Mamohela</td></tr>
<tr><td>1870–1</td><td>**July–February.** Ill at Bambarre</td></tr>
<tr><td>1871</td><td>**April–June.** At Nyangwe village
5 November. Arrives at Ujiji
10 November. Henry M. Stanley arrives at Ujiji</td></tr>
<tr><td>1872</td><td>**March–August.** Stays at Unyanyembe
14 August. Leaves Unyanyembe on final journey</td></tr>
<tr><td>1873</td><td>**January.** Journey in swamps beside Lake Bangweulu</td></tr>
<tr><td>1873</td><td>**1 May.** Dies at Chitambo's village</td></tr>
<tr><td>1874</td><td>**February.** Livingstone's body reaches Zanzibar
18 April. Funeral and interment at Westminster Abbey, London</td></tr>
</table>

LIVINGSTONE'S EARLY LIFE

Worthy but remote from brilliant[1]

On 19 March 1813, at Shuttle Row in the Scottish village of Blantyre, Lanarkshire, a second child was born to Agnes Hunter and her husband Neil Livingston, a self-employed commercial traveller in tea. The birth took place in a three-storey tenement block,[2] which was the staff housing for the adjacent Blantyre Works, a cotton spinning mill. Neil's father (also Neil) had a responsible position as handler of the mill's cash, having been forced from his croft on the island of Ulva during the Highland clearances, after the Battle of Culloden in 1746.

Neil and Agnes Livingston had seven children, of whom five survived – John, David, Charles, Agnes and Janet. The family spelled their surname without the final 'e', as did David until 1857.[3] They lived in a tiny top-floor apartment in Shuttle Row, a dwelling they had inherited from Agnes's father. It was probably to retain the apartment that John and David were put to work in the mill at the age of ten, because their father, who was not an employee of Monteith & Co., the owners, had no real right to be there. David worked fourteen-hour days as a piecer — a lad who moved round the spinning machines repairing thread. When the mill closed at 8 p.m. there were two hours of schooling, provided by the mill owners for their child workers. The owners also supplied a library for their staff.

Because David's father had given him lessons he was literate when he started his schooling at the mill. He used part of his first pay packet to buy a Latin grammar, which he took to work with him each day, glancing at it whenever he had a chance. This cannot have endeared him to the other child workers, but David developed the obstinacy which was to serve him so well in his later life, and tried to ignore their taunts. When his body had grown large enough, he was promoted to spinner, at the age of nineteen. Altogether he spent sixteen years working in the mill.

We cannot know for sure what books David read in his adolescence, although his father, a member of the Independent Congregational Church, preferred religious tracts and devotional works. The mill library may well have contained the accounts of exploration written by travellers of the late eighteenth and early nineteenth centuries, such as Mungo Park, Hugh

Clapperton and James Bruce (Africa) and Matthew Flinders (Australia). In 1834 Neil Livingston brought home from church a pamphlet written by Karl von Gutzlaff, a missionary in China, exhorting young men to become medical missionaries there. This had a profound effect on David, who may already have been contemplating a medical career. He had become interested in science, to the dismay of his father, who could not reconcile the subject with his religious beliefs. Now, as a spinner, David was earning enough to put by some savings. It took him eighteen months to save the requisite sum for entry in 1836 to Anderson's College, Glasgow, to begin studying medicine at the age of twenty-three.

During vacations, Livingstone (to help the reader, a final 'e' will be attached to his name long before he himself made the change) returned to Blantyre, eight miles from Glasgow, to work in the mill. After two years of medical studies, he applied to join the London Missionary Society, a non-denominational but mostly Congregational body. In August 1838 he was sent for training at the LMS seminary at Chipping Ongar, Essex. With his thick Scottish accent, curious swallowing delivery and staccato bursts of speech, and slow comprehension due to having been largely self-taught, he did not impress his tutors or fellow students. His tutor Richard Cecil thought him 'worthy but remote from brilliant'. His reserve was misinterpreted as sullenness and his undoubted application and seriousness as lack of humour. His looks were also to his disadvantage. Five feet eight inches tall, with a face already showing the first signs of deep vertical lines either side of a turned-down mouth, he appeared to be a man whose spirit was as gloomy and dark as his hair and eyes. He was obsessed with his bowel movements, an interest he was to retain throughout his life.

None the less, young men willing to become medical missionaries were hard to come by, and the LMS paid for Livingstone's third and final year of medical study, which he undertook in London. He successfully took his medical degree in Glasgow, and was ordained on 20 November 1840. His dream of going to China was shattered by the outbreak of the Opium War; instead, the LMS decided to send him to South Africa. He boarded the barque *George* on 8 December 1840, suffered a rough crossing of the Bay of Biscay ('imagine if you can a ship in a fit of epilepsy'[4]) and arrived in Simon's Bay at the southern tip of Africa on 15 March 1841. 'Everything', said Livingstone, 'is so different from the idea I formed of them while reading. The actual sight and the imagination are two very different things. This is really a fine world we live in, after all.'[5]

While still in London in 1840, Livingstone had met Robert Moffat, who had established a mission station at Kuruman, in the interior of Africa, beyond Cape Colony. It was there that Livingstone was bound. After a journey of 600 miles by ox wagon, he arrived at Moffat's mission station on 31 July 1841. Moffat, still absent, had advised Livingstone to learn the Setswana language, on which he had made a start on the boat. In order further to immerse himself in the language, and bored with Kuruman, which was set in a landscape of dry scrub, Livingstone joined a lay missionary, Rogers Edwards, on a trip northwards to spy out the land for a new mission. He also began the habit of writing copious letters. His correspondence is enormous, for his letters were seldom less than 1,500 words long.

This 1841 journey, covering 700 miles altogether, was a catalyst in Livingstone's life. He had been surprised that Kuruman had only forty converts after twenty years of missionary labour, and it dawned on him that missionaries and the mission societies must exaggerate the numbers of conversions in order to keep funds flowing. In truth, there was little for him to do in Kuruman, and inactivity was anathema to this auto-didact. 'There is a lamentable deadness prevailing in the whole of this field – there are no conversions the [*sic*] only work proceeding with anything like briskness is [Moffat's] translation of the Bible into the language of

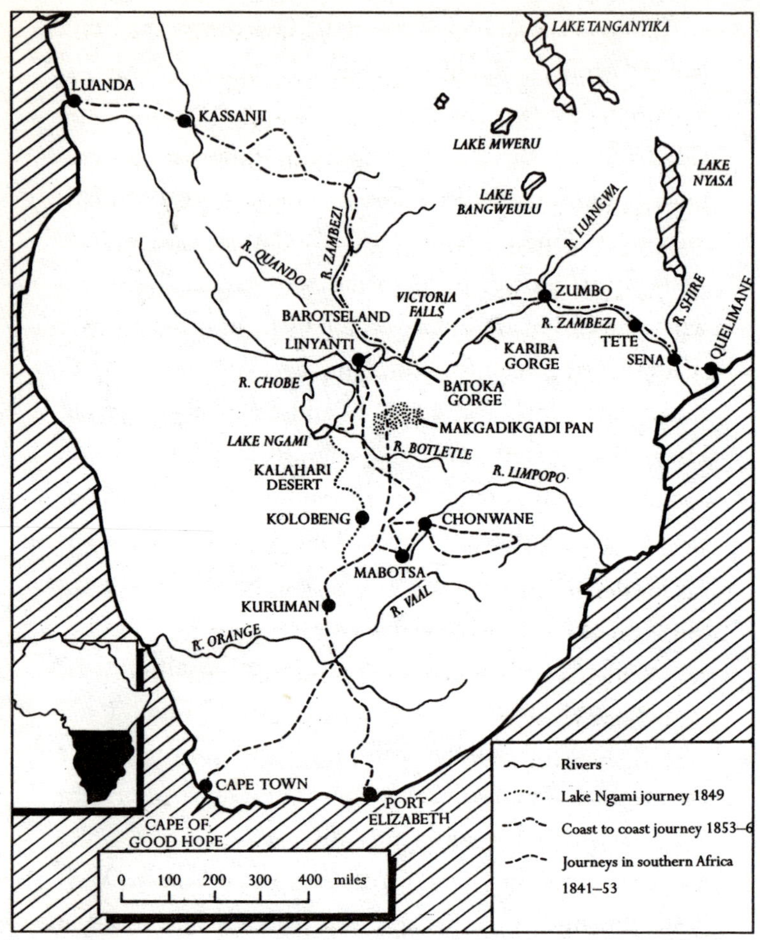

Livingstone's Journeys 1841–1856

the people.'[6] Livingstone had been shocked by the number of missionaries working close together in Cape Colony. He believed that the proper function of a missionary was to work with people hitherto beyond Christianity's reach. Once a church had been established, it should be self-governing under an African pastor, and the missionaries should then travel to a heathen tribe. 'An onward movement ought to be made, whether men will hear or they will forebear.'[7]

Livingstone undertook two more northward journeys, in 1842 and 1843, reaching the south-west border of modern Zimbabwe. On the way he wore a peaked cap which was to become his trademark. This was modelled on a naval cap worn by the captain of the *George* on the way to South Africa. The upper part was well padded as protection against the sun, and there was a gold band around the rim.[8]

His companions on the journeys were Tswana servants from Kuruman, in whose customs, language and way of thinking Livingstone could steep himself on the way. Perhaps because he was a Scot who felt some alienation from the English, or because he was a man of humble origins, Livingstone respected his African companions and treated them, if not as equals, at least as worthy of tolerance and understanding. At first, he held the traditional missionary view that 'these degraded beings we hope to raise to the level of humanity and civilization'.[9] Soon, however, he developed unpatronizing and open-minded attitudes which were unusual at the time, when the notion of white, and particularly British, supremacy was already well established. He can be contrasted with a contemporary explorer, Richard Burton, who believed that 'the negro, in mass, will not improve beyond a certain point, and that not respectable. He mentally remains a child.'[10] Livingstone saw that various 'heathen' habits and attitudes had a social purpose, and he sometimes felt that Africans were harmed, rather than helped, by contact with Europeans. None the less, he remained always convinced that Christianity had paramount virtues, which gave his work meaning.

Livingstone got on well with his black travelling companions, but he was critical and intolerant of whites. Perhaps he felt comfortable with blacks because he did not see them as threats. He would have been unaware of criticism from people speaking a language he only half-understood, and he could not be sensitive to social nuances in a way of life so different from his own. It was easier and more comfortable for this socially inept man to be with black people.

His attitude towards Africans was more akin to that of French, rather than British, missionaries. French Huguenot missionaries had already established themselves in the area that has become Lesotho, 600 miles south-east of Kuruman. Two of them had written a book of their travels, which mentioned a large lake in the interior. Moffat had also heard of this lake, which was called Ngami, and at some stage Livingstone's interest was aroused. First, however, he tried to establish three missions, all of them failures. With Rogers Edwards he set up a station at Mabotsa, 250 miles north-east of Kuruman, but the two men soon quarrelled, and Livingstone was attacked by a lion, which gripped his left upper arm in its jaws before it was killed by an African companion. 'I walked home without assistance. . . . The excessive discharge however soon reduced me to a skeleton.'[11] This necessitated him recuperating in Kuruman. Livingstone then moved 40 miles to the north to build a mission at Chonwane (about 40 miles north of today's Zeerust), this time with a wife.

Mary, Robert Moffat's eldest daughter, got to know Livingstone during his convalescence at Kuruman, which took several months, for, although he had set his own bone, it failed to heal properly. Later he damaged it again when building a house. Many years later his body was identified by this misshapen arm. Mary was twenty-three, no beauty, with black hair and a short, stout body. On Livingstone's side, the marriage, performed at

Kuruman on 2 January 1845, was a match of convenience, rather than love, although he did later develop love for his wife. Mary had been brought up in Africa and went to school there. A fluent speaker of Setswana, she wanted to follow her husband on his travels. At first they tried to set up home in Mabotsa, but relations with Edwards and his wife became impossible. Livingstone and Mary then went to Chonwane. They remained there for less than a year, during which time Mary gave birth to a son, Robert.

Livingstone was a poor preacher. His plan was to convert the local leader, Sechele, so that his people would follow him into Christianity. There was a lack of water at Chonwane, so in 1847 Sechele and his people moved 80 miles north to Kolobeng, near Gaborone, the present-day capital of Botswana, and Livingstone's family followed (the ruins of the house he built there can still be seen). They stayed for four years. Sechele was baptized in September 1848, having promised to give up three of his wives. When Livingstone discovered the chief had resumed relations with one of them in March the following year, he was bitterly disappointed. He was never to make another conversion. Meanwhile, Mary baked bread in an anthill her husband had hollowed out, and started an infant school, which she gave up when Thomas was born.

An idea, the seeds of which had already been planted, was taking root in Livingstone's mind. He could travel in the interior of Africa, sending back information which would enable commerce to be established with its inhabitants. Their lands would thus be 'opened out', crops such as cotton – memories of his childhood work in a cotton factory never left him – could be planted, and Christianity would follow when the Africans' minds had been made more receptive by their contact with the outside world. He put this plan to the LMS, because he had to retain his means of livelihood, the £100 a year they paid him.

Already there were two types of occasional visitors to his area – the traders and the big-game hunters. He had met one of the latter in 1843 at Mabotsa: Thomas Steele, of the Indian Army. Two further visitors from India, Frank Vardon and William Cotton Oswell, based themselves at Mabotsa in 1845, while they went shooting and exploring to the north-east. Oswell was rich and able to make a repeat visit in 1848, with Mungo Murray, a Scottish aristocrat, and J.H. Wilson, a trader searching for ivory. When the group reached Kolobeng in late 1849, Livingstone decided to join them, to look for the oft-reported Lake Ngami, which two previous white expeditions had failed to reach, driven back by the Kalahari (now Kgaligadi) desert. With the advantage of having with them the Setswana-speaker Livingstone and a Tswana who had been to the lake before, the group travelled 600 miles in nine weeks, reaching the lake, which stretched beyond the horizon, on 1 August 1849. Livingstone commented on the slow progress of travel: 'The great drawback to travelling in this country is the slowness of our locomotives. The heavy lumbering Dutch waggon and the riding ox are the only conveyances unless we choose to try our own lower extremities.'[12]

Rightly or wrongly, Livingstone took the credit for the 'discovery' of Lake Ngami. When he returned to Kolobeng, he wrote to the LMS about the journey, and they passed his letter to the Royal Geographical Society, which had been founded in 1830, with the purpose of being closely associated with exploration and travel. After the expansion into the Indian subcontinent in the latter half of the eighteenth century, the next vast unexplored area was Africa, which had had European settlements around its periphery for centuries, but whose interior was still largely unmapped. Victorian Britain was as interested in the exploration of Africa as, a little over a century later, the whole world would be in the journey to, and landing on, the moon. The RGS awarded Livingstone its gold medal and twenty-five guineas. His name was now known, and Livingstone found this much to his liking.

Livingstone was an ambitious man. Someone who had developed from being a factory boy at the age of ten, to a literate teenager, to a young man with a medical degree who had also been ordained, to a traveller and missionary in Africa who was able to describe his exploration in a manner which won him an RGS gold medal, could not be anything less. His ambition was now fed by his acclaim. This was better than being a missionary, stuck in an outpost in Africa attempting to Christianize people profoundly reluctant to listen and alter their entire culture. The feeling of uselessness could be set aside when a life of exploration beckoned.

The white men who in 1849 had visited Lake Ngami, which is now little more than a marsh on the edge of the vast Okavango swamp, had been prevented from going further because they had no boat which could cross the Botletle river. Oswell decided to go back to the Cape to buy one. He returned to Kolobeng with it in May 1850, by which time Livingstone had already left, taking northward with him his family, which now consisted of Mary, Robert (four), Agnes (three), and Thomas (a baby). Mary, yet again pregnant, had probably refused to let her husband disappear once more on a long journey. We must also remember that she had been in Africa for many years, and what seemed to the English at home as a trek into the unknown must not have appeared that way to the Livingstones. The African peoples in the area had contacts with their neighbours, information derived from word of mouth enabled the white family to know where they were going and many of the hazards that would be encountered, and native guides could always be acquired.

The second Ngami journey, whose purpose was to find a way to the Zambezi river, was not a success. When the Livingstones reached the lake they were bitten by mosquitoes and developed malaria. The oxen pulling their wagon were attacked by tsetse flies. With Mary's confinement imminent, the family returned to Kolobeng. A daughter, Elizabeth, was born, only to die six weeks later; her grave can still be seen. The trip had shown that the Ngami route was not suitable as a means of reaching the Zambezi.

Livingstone determined to go north a third time, with his family and Oswell, and they all departed in April 1851. Mary was again pregnant. Her mother was furious with Livingstone: 'Will you again expose her and them in these sickly regions on an exploring expedition. All the world will condemn the cruelty of the thing. A pregnant woman with three little children trailing about with a company of the other sex through the wilds of Africa among savage men and beasts.'[13] This time they travelled due north across the Botletle river and the great Makgadikgadi salt pan, to the Linyanti swamps. On the way two baobab trees stand out starkly in the desert; they are now known as 'Green's baobabs', because Frederick and Charles Green, who passed that way the following year, carved the words 'Green's expedition' on the smaller. Livingstone measured its diameter, and today it measures a few centimetres less. It also bears the date 1771 and the name and date Hendrik van Zyl 1851. Neither of these was mentioned by Livingstone. Van Zyl may have been a Boer hunter from the Transvaal who travelled that way later in the year. The date 1771 is either a hoax, or a trader (possibly a Portuguese from the coast?) may have visited the area.

Mary and the children were left at Linyanti (sometimes called Dinyanti, but long ago abandoned), while Oswell and Livingstone paddled by canoe to the Chobe river. They met the chief of the Kololo people, Sebitwane, who died of a lung infection a few days later. They then travelled along and mapped the local waterways, proving that the Chobe joined the Zambezi. Oswell urged Livingstone to return to Mary, who gave birth to a son, (William) Oswell, on the banks of the Botletle (or Boteti river, called by Livingstone the Zouga, after a nearby chief), where they stayed a month to allow the mother to rest.

When they returned to Kolobeng the mission was deserted. Sechele had moved 10 miles away to a place which had more water. Thus collapsed Livingstone's third mission station in Africa. Failure can, however, be as important as success. Livingstone learned a great deal in these years, particularly about how to manage malaria, against which he developed a prophylactive and curative system whose importance cannot be too highly stressed. He was able to stay alive in Africa when other white men perished. He obtained a copy of the *Medical History of the Expedition to the Niger during the Years 1841–2* by James Ormiston, and kept himself aware of new medical discoveries by having sent to him the *British and Foreign Medical Review* and the *Lancet*. Later he was to give quinine wine (two grains of quinine steeped in sherry) to European companions every day, and he developed his own pill for malaria, which he administered as soon as the first symptoms appeared. It was composed of quinine, rhubarb, resin of jalap, calomel and spirit of cardamoms. The patient was to be dosed until the ears rang or deafness ensued.[14]

ACROSS AFRICA, 1852–6

Aye put a stout heart to a steye brae [Always put a stout heart to a steep declivity][1]

With Kolobeng deserted, Livingstone had to decide on his own future and that of his family. He determined to send his wife and children home to Scotland to live with his parents, while he made preparations at Cape Town for another great journey. The idea for this latest exploration had come to him during the recent trek to the Zambezi with Oswell. Sebitwane's people, the Kololo, spoke Sesutho, a language very similar to Setswana; Livingstone had found no difficulty in understanding them or making himself understood. Despite his previous belief that the Kololo 'are just such a strange mixture of good and evil as men are everywhere else',[2] he began to condemn their tribalism, claiming that they would only become civilized 'by a long and continued discipline and contact with superior races by commerce'.[3] Only when tribal collectivism had been weakened by western trading methods would they be in a more receptive state of mind to appreciate the foreign Christian faith.[4]

They also inhabited an area to the west of the Zambezi (present-day Barotseland), parts of which he thought would be high in altitude and therefore free of tsetse fly and malaria. Moreover, they used cloth which had been transported from the Portuguese settlements of the west coast of Africa, and therefore must be accustomed to trading. It looked as though the route from their land to the west coast would be easier to traverse than making the long trek up from the south through the Kalahari desert; the matter deserved investigation. The presence of the Zambezi also gave them permanent water for crops. All these factors augured well for the development of trade, since the Kololo already indulged in it, and therefore for the establishment of missions.

Another factor now influenced Livingstone's thinking. He had heard from the Kololo that the cloth trade was inseparable from the ivory and slave trades between the coast and the interior. His campaign against the iniquities of the slave trade was about to begin.

First, he despatched his family to Scotland by ship on 23 April 1852. He was not to see them again for four and a half years. Oswell paid their fares and also gave Livingstone £200, with which he equipped himself for his journey, using part of it to pay for the surgical removal of his uvula in Cape Town in March. The operation did not seem to make his speech much clearer. He also purchased a chronometer and was taught to take latitude and longitude correctly by the astronomer royal at the Cape. He had already had lessons in navigation from the captain of the ship which had originally taken him to Africa in 1841.

At the beginning of June 1852 he left Cape Town, reaching Kuruman in August. There he was joined by George Fleming, a freed West Indian slave, and some African drivers. The trekkers reached the main Kololo settlement at Linyanti on 23 May 1853, having bypassed Boers who had attacked Sechele, killed more than a hundred of his Kwena people, and sacked Livingstone's former house at Kolobeng. The Boers were very suspicious of the English missionaries, whom they regarded as dangerous rivals for land and influence. Livingstone detested them: 'They look upon themselves as the peculiar favourites of Heaven – that they resemble the children of Israel when led by Moses. And the blacks are the descendants of Cain – and may be shot as so many baboons.'[5]

Sekeletu, a successor to Sebitwane as leader of the Kololo, took Livingstone's party 200 miles from Linyanti up the Zambezi by canoe, leaving them to travel a further hundred miles upstream by themselves.

Livingstone was searching for a spot free from malaria and tsetse fly for a trading station and mission; seven attacks of fever made him return to Linyanti, having failed to find a suitable site.

Worried about his failure, Livingstone wrote from Linyanti on 24 September 1853 to ask whether the British government might lend him its support. He had mapped the upper Zambezi with accurate latitudes and longitudes, unlike the Portuguese traders from the Atlantic coast and Arab traders from the East African coast, who were already in the region in search of ivory and slaves. Livingstone had met on the upper Zambezi Silva Porto, a Portuguese trader who claimed to have crossed Africa from the Portuguese Atlantic coast to the Portuguese East African coast, and Arab traders from Zanzibar. Partly to investigate trade in the region, partly to map the area properly, and probably partly to reach a coast where he could despatch letters, he determined to make for Luanda, the Portuguese capital on the Atlantic coast.

Sekeletu provided him with oxen and twenty-seven porters, and the party departed Linyanti on 11 November 1853. After they left the Barotseland plain, they entered forest during the rainy season. There were swarms of mosquitoes, whose connexion with malaria was as yet unknown, and tsetse flies, whose ability to kill animals was recognized. They passed through the lands of the Lunda people, who were friendly, and the Chokwe, who were hostile. Eventually they reached the settlement of Kassanji, 300 miles from the coast, the Portuguese village furthest in the interior. Da Silva Rega, the commandant, took the party under his wing, provided them with food and shelter, and assisted in the purchase of supplies for the rest of the journey, with ivory which Sekeletu had given Livingstone.

Six weeks after leaving Kassanji, Livingstone reached Luanda at the end of May 1854. He was by then so ill with diarrhoea and fever that the sole British resident in the town, Edmund Gabriel, the British commissioner for the suppression of the slave trade, took him into his house and gave him the care he required. The Kololo porters were also given assistance. It took two months for Livingstone to recover.

It is strange that Livingstone did not then embark on a ship for either Europe or South Africa. He may have thought that he had failed in his objective of discovering a site for a mission station; he may have wished to return the loyal Kololo porters to their homeland; perhaps he wanted to be the first man from Britain to cross the African continent – he knew that Arabs and at least one Portuguese had already done so. Possibly he aimed further to examine the slave and closely linked ivory trades. The notion that he was now an explorer was confirmed by his detailed descriptions of his journeys. As an explorer, his ambition must be to be first, and he was alarmed to be asked to take with him the Austrian botanist Federeich Welwitz, sent from Lisbon to explore Angola. He refused to do so, lest the Austrian report back to Europe before him. He must now hurry.

He set off from Luanda on 20 September 1854, reaching Linyanti in August 1855. His plan was to follow the Zambezi to the east coast. He had heard that several miles to the east the river became unnavigable because of the existence of a great waterfall, but it might be navigable thereafter. He departed, with a party numbering about 200, on 3 November 1855, again having been given provisions and porters by Sekeletu. On 16 November he reached the mile-wide and 300-feet deep waterfall called by the Kololo 'Mosi-oa-tunya', or 'the smoke that thunders'. He was paddled to an island in the middle of the river (now called Livingstone Island), from which he could lean over the edge to see the falls to his left and right. The falls are particularly impressive because they descend into a narrow canyon, the sides of which are the same height. It is this which causes the water to bounce up in spray 450 yards above the ground, spray which is visible for miles around and easily mistaken for smoke. The thundering sound of the water's fall is also magnified by the narrowness of the cavern into which it falls.

Livingstone's description of what he saw displays his wonder:

> I did not comprehend it until, creeping with awe to the verge, I peered down into a large rent which had been made from bank to bank of the broad Zambesi, and saw that a stream a thousand yards broad leaped down a hundred feet and then became suddenly compressed into a space of fifteen or twenty yards. . . . The snow white sheet seemed like myriads of small comets all rushing in one direction, each of which left behind its nucleus rays of foam. . . . It had never before been seen by European eyes, but scenes so lovely must have been gazed upon by angels in their flight.[6]

Livingstone called the vast waterfall Victoria Falls, after his queen. He cut his initials and the date 1855 on a tree on the island. 'This is the only instance in which I indulged in this piece of vanity.'[7] He also planted a hundred peach and apricot stones and a quantity of coffee seeds, but the saplings were destroyed by hippos. The tree on which he carved his initials no longer exists.

The Zambezi does an abrupt acute-angled turn here, where the river appears to boil in a cauldron. It then follows the 70-mile long zigzagging Batoka gorge. What caused this geographical phenomenon? The Zambezi river once flowed south into the Limpopo river, but it was trapped by the southernmost arm of the Great Rift Valley, when large-scale earth movements, probably caused by the shifting of tectonic plates, fractured what is now northern Botswana and adjoining areas in Zambia, Namibia and Zimbabwe. There was an outpouring of lava and a faulting of the earth's surface, which caused the Batoka gorge and the many cross-faults into which the Zambezi cut successive cataracts. The river gouged out the soft material that had accumulated in these faults, but not the solid bedrock. It thus created what is probably the world's greatest showpiece, a majestic curtain of falling water.

Livingstone now left the Zambezi, travelling northwards in search of his healthy high ground for a mission station. This northward loop brought him to the Kafue river, which he followed downstream until it joined the Zambezi. By doing this he unfortunately missed the Kariba gorge, which made the Zambezi unnavigable in the area. Ignorant of that feature, he determined to follow the Zambezi to the sea, and return with a boat which he would sail up the river, thus showing it was navigable, a suitable conduit for trade, and an easy means of getting to the interior, which would therefore be much more accessible from the east coast of Africa than the west. He came across another obstacle, the Mpata gorge, but he skirted it on foot. He then reached the confluence of the Luangwa river and the Zambezi, where there was a ruined Portuguese settlement called Zumbo. This was the furthest inland that the Portuguese from the east coast of Africa had settled. There he was advised to avoid difficult country by striking across land to Tete, where he would meet the Zambezi again. By following this counsel, Livingstone made his second big mistake: he missed the Cabora Bassa rapids, which also make the Zambezi unnavigable. He left most of his Kololo porters at Tete, assuring them that he would return to restore them to their homeland, and paddled downriver before walking overland to his final destination – Quelimane, an east coast town occupied by the Portuguese.

He arrived at Quelimane on 20 May 1856, four years after he had quit Cape Town. There he found the Royal Navy awaiting him with supplies and letters. They had been told of his journey by Edmund Gabriel, with whom he had stayed in Luanda. He was taken to the British island of Mauritius, where he rested for two months. He then took the northward route via the Red Sea to Marseille, and thence travelled overland through France and back to England.

One of the letters Livingstone had received at Quelimane was from the LMS, saying they did not consider his travels as missionary activity, and they disagreed with his suggestion that a mission be established in central Africa. Livingstone would have been dismayed by this had not a letter simultaneously arrived from the chairman of the Royal Geographical Society, Sir Roderick Murchison, praising his activities. From his reception at Quelimane and Mauritius he was made aware that he was now famous because of his journey to Luanda – as yet, Europe was ignorant of the transcontinental crossing. He therefore thought he might obtain support elsewhere, even though this might necessitate his resignation from the LMS.

What had Livingstone achieved by his trans-African journey? The geographical exploration, careful mapping, taking of positions of latitude and longitude, and detailed journal entries – later published – were a great scientific achievement. Due to his bravery, which often lapsed into foolhardiness, he had performed an extraordinary physical feat, travelling across Africa on foot, by oxen, and by boat. He provided the West with descriptions of the peoples of the interior of Africa and their societies and methods of government, a prerequisite for European expansion into the interior and the setting of the stage for the later imperial rivalries. He had also brought to the attention of the British people the realities of the operation of the slave trade in central Africa, describing the slave-holding African societies and the way they sold slaves to Arab or Portuguese merchants, or attacked neighbouring societies to obtain slaves to barter for cloth, beads and guns. He argued that legitimate trade should replace this traffic in human flesh.

As regards his failures, Livingstone did not convince any Africans to adopt Christianity, though he preached to many people in the course of his journeys. He also failed to find a suitable site for a mission, despite his later irresponsible advocacy of various places in the interior.

FAME AND FAMILY

A cold shiver comes over me when I think of my speech at which
I am labouring[1]

When Livingstone reached London from Paris, on 10 December 1856, he found that Mary, expecting him to arrive at Southampton by boat, had gone there to meet him. He hurried down to Southampton himself, to be greeted by his wife and presented with a poem she had written, of which the final verse read:

> You'll never part me darling, there's a promise in
>   your eye;
> I may tend you while I'm living, you will watch me
>   when I die;
> And if death but kindly lead me to the blessed home
>   on high,
> What a hundred thousand welcomes will await you in
>   the sky.[2]

Mary had not seen her husband for four and a half years. When she returned to England from the Cape of Good

Hope in 1852, she went to stay with her parents-in-law in Scotland. Neil Livingston had moved to a small cottage in Hamilton with his wife and two daughters, who carried on a millinery business from that address, and there was little space for Mary and her four children, who ranged in age from six years to one.

None the less, the fatherless family was made welcome. The strain of living in such crowded and confined quarters soon began to tell, however, and after six months Mary left Hamilton. She went with her children to Hackney in London, to the house of friends of her father. She then moved from one lodging house to another, always short of money, and with one or other of the children, particularly Tom, who always ill (it has been suggested that he had contracted bilharzia in Africa and this was the cause of his distressing symptoms, although when he died, as a young adult, a doctor thought his death was due to Bright's disease). She had very limited financial resources: the LMS gave her £30 a quarter, which she could not manage on. She repeatedly asked them for advances. Livingstone later accused the LMS of not paying her the correct amounts due from his allowance. She was not receiving letters from her husband, then in the African interior, or any news of him, and she had nothing to relieve the strain of loneliness and of looking after four young children. She moved to Manchester, but then found a haven in the

Lake District, at the home of the Braithwaite family, Quakers who lived at Kendal. Mrs Braithwaite was herself a missionary wife, able to understand the difficulties of being parted from a husband. Mary suffered a breakdown in the winter of 1853/4, and also became physically ill. She had somewhat recovered by the spring of 1854, but news from Luanda that David was going back into the interior cast her into gloom. She moved south, to Epsom, in the summer of 1854.

When her husband returned, she had to share him with the adulation of the British public, spearheaded by Sir Roderick Murchison, president of the Royal Geographical Society. On 15 December 1856 there was an official reception at the RGS, at which Livingstone was awarded their Victoria Medal. The following day they attended a meeting at the LMS, a less happy occasion because of the society's reluctance to view Livingstone's wanderings as missionary activity, despite the argument that they were a prelude to evangelization. Prince Albert also received Livingstone, a sure indication that he was now a public figure. There was no mention of the Portuguese contribution to the exploration or crossing of Africa from west to east; perhaps the British were ignorant of this. If so, they were soon reminded of what the Portuguese had done. At the instigation of the Portuguese government, José de Lacerda wrote articles in the *Diario de Lisboa* of

15, 17 and 19 December 1864 (these were translated into English and issued as a pamphlet in London). However convincing the arguments, it was to a Britain confident of its own superiority to which Livingstone had returned – to a country already largely covered with railways and financing and laying rail in South America, a country which had held the Great Exhibition of 1851, a land in which the discoveries of Charles Darwin (*Voyage of the Beagle*, reissued in 1845) and Richard Burton (*Personal Narrative of a Pilgrimage to El-Medinah and Meccah*, 1855) were being propagated.

Livingstone's father had died recently, and David and Mary went to Hamilton to see his mother and sisters. On their return to London, Livingstone undertook negotiations with John Murray, the official publisher to the RGS, for a book about his life. On 22 January 1857, at 57 Sloane Street, London, the explorer sat down to write *Missionary Travels and Researches in South Africa*. He and Mary settled with the children at a small house at Hadley Green, just north of London, and for the first time in five years he could play with his children.

Livingstone's *Missionary Travels* seems at times to have been written by a different person from the one who had been sending home despatches to the LMS and letters to friends over the previous sixteen years. Safely ensconced in London, he conveniently forgot the immense difficulties he had faced in trying to convert Africans to the Christian faith, and his narrative gives his actions and travels one purpose – to bring the Word to the heathen African. He had to justify himself and leave the door open for support for further journeys. The book also contains careful and beautiful descriptions of nature. It was a great success, containing as it did stories of daring deeds for the armchair explorer, descriptions of the way of life of Africans for the white supremacist, mapping for the cartographer, potential new fields of endeavour for the Christian missionary, rich pickings for the merchant, fertile land for the farming settler, and further work for the anti-slaver. The book was published in November 1857, with a first printing of 12,000 copies. Before publication, it had been oversubscribed at a guinea a copy (at the time, books were announced and people paid for them before publication) and later printings sold another 58,000 copies. Livingstone was able to deposit over £9,000 in the bank. With this, his family's financial problems were solved: he set up a trust fund for his children.

The book was completed at the end of July 1857, and Livingstone had to review his future. We have seen how, when he was travelling to the east coast of Africa along the Zambezi in 1855, he determined to return with a boat to establish the navigability of the river from the coast to the interior, where a mission might be built. He also hoped to replace the slave trade with legitimate commerce. At a meeting in Cambridge town hall, he said:

> I propose in my next expedition to visit the Zambesi, and to propitiate the different chiefs along its banks, endeavouring to induce them to cultivate cotton, and to abolish the slave-trade: already they trade in ivory and gold-dust, and are anxious to extend their commercial operations. There is thus a probability of their interests being linked with ours, and thus the elevation of the African would be the result.[3]

As the LMS seemed reluctant to support him, he began to look elsewhere for funds.

His fame had spread throughout Britain. He had been given the freedom of the cities of London, Glasgow and Edinburgh, had been elected a Fellow of the Royal Society, had addressed chambers of commerce and cotton associations in Manchester, Dundee, Halifax, Liverpool and Leeds. Livingstone intensely disliked public speaking. 'He had rather a peculiar accent in talking, and still more in reading, English. It almost seemed foreign, or as if the language were not quite familiar to him, and did not run from his tongue naturally.'[4] 'His language was peculiar to himself — short jerky sentences, expressive of thoughts which he could not arrange in set periods.'[5] On 13 February he went to tea with Queen Victoria in Buckingham Palace. He was taken up by the philanthropist Miss Coutts, who bought him a microscope.

When he was at Quelimane in 1856, he had received Murchison's letter of congratulations. Indeed Murchison, who was a firm believer in the exploratory aspect of Livingstone's travels, wrote to Lord Clarendon, the British Foreign Secretary, requesting his assistance. There was a precedent for this: in 1856 Richard Burton and John Hanning Speke had departed on their expedition to the lakes of central Africa via Zanzibar, an island off Africa's east coast, sponsored by both the RGS and the Foreign Office. Murchison stressed the paradise of wealth – agricultural and mineral – on the upper Zambezi, and suggested that Britain should negotiate with the Portuguese over acquiring this area. As a result, Livingstone was appointed a roving British consul, with an annual salary of £500, in a region which included Mozambique and a large tranche of territory to the west. The House of Commons was told on 11 December 1857 about Livingstone's commission to lead a government-sponsored expedition to the Zambezi, and on the following day the explorer was entertained to lunch at 10 Downing Street by the Prime Minister, Lord Palmerston.

The Portuguese were naturally most unhappy at this development: they did not want a British expedition sailing up the Zambezi to establish British influence in the interior, for they had maintained an unrealized hope that one day their possessions in east and west Africa would be united in the centre, and they would have a band of territory from coast to coast. They refused to accept Livingstone's appointment as consul at Sena and Tete, inland on the Zambezi, and allowed him to be consul only at Quelimane. This was unacceptable to the explorer, who persuaded the Foreign Office to make him consul at Quelimane, Barotseland (the area in the middle of Africa where the Kololo lived), and other African chieftainships beyond the limit of Portuguese claims. This appointment lasted from 22 February 1858 to 1864. Portugal, anticipating difficulties when Livingstone reached Africa, tried to prevent them by abolishing slavery in Portuguese territory, with the caveat that this rule would not come into effect for twenty years.

Government support led to the enlargement of Livingtone's ambitions. For the first time, we learn of one of his covert hopes; he wrote to Professor Adam Sedgwick of Cambridge, describing the men he was taking with him – a mining geologist to examine mineral resources, an economic botanist, an artist, a naval officer, and a moral agent to lay Christian foundations – ostensibly for developing African trade and promoting civilization, 'but what I tell to none but such as you in whom I have confidence is thus I hope it may result in an English colony in the healthy highlands of Central Africa'.[6] His previous ideas of the inseparability of commerce and Christianity, which would result in civilization, had secretly developed into settlement, commerce and Christianity.

A week before *Missionary Travels* was published Livingstone resigned from the LMS. This was a mixed blessing for the society. On the one hand his public fame was an asset when appealing for funds – over £6,000 had been raised for a Barotseland mission – but, on the other, his evangelizing rather than travelling was what they were paying him for. Livingstone had been advocating the establishment of a mission in Barotseland as a reason for his travels, despite the fact that he had failed to find any healthy highlands there, free from malaria and tsetse flies. This was unwise in the extreme and tantamount to sending people to their deaths. Livingstone was also advocating the building of another mission, further east among the Ndebele in what is now Zimbabwe. He ended one of his Cambridge lectures with the rousing words: 'I beg to direct your attention to Africa; – I know that in a few years I shall be cut off in that country, which is now open; do not let it be shut again! I go back to Africa to make an open path for commerce and Christianity; do you carry out the work which I have begun. *I leave it with you!*'[7] It is these words which were responsible for the formation of the Universities' Mission to Central Africa, an Anglican group supported by Cambridge, Oxford, Durham and Trinity College in Dublin.

When Parliament voted £5,000 for the expedition, Livingstone began to order supplies and gather staff, under the aegis of Captain John Washington of the Royal Navy. He later complained that 'most of the money spent on this expedition has not been on objects primarily in view but in birds beetles and pebbles. The great scientific men crowded around me when it was known I was going out and everyone had a claim for a man in his speciality.'[8] Mary insisted on accompanying him on this expedition, although she decided to take only one of their children, six-year-old Oswell. Agnes, now eleven, would stay in Hamilton with her aunts and grandmother, who would be paid an allowance, and Robert (nearly twelve) and Tom (nine) would be placed in schools. The three children left behind were to be under the care of trustees, who would pay for their upkeep and education from the profits of *Missionary Travels*. An unofficial trustee, Bevan Braithwaite of Kendal, was to take a personal interest in the children. It was at his home that the Livingstones spent their last night in England and at Kendal station that they waved goodbye to their children, en route for Birkenhead, where they were to embark on their ship *Pearl*, the Colonial Office steamship.

The other members of Livingstone's expedition were Captain Norman Bedingfeld of the Royal Navy, who was in charge of the small steamer which had been loaded on to the *Pearl* in pieces, to be reassembled at the mouth of the Zambezi prior to steaming up it; Dr John Kirk, a Scot who had practised as a doctor in the recent Crimean War and who was an experienced botanist; Livingstone's younger brother Charles, a Nonconformist minister, who had been a pastor in New York and New England from 1849 to 1857, and had come over from the United States to help as an amanuensis for *Missionary Travels* – he was to be a photographer and 'moral agent'; Richard Thornton, a geologist; Thomas Baines, the expedition's official artist; and George Rae, another Scot, who was an engineer. In a letter to Thornton, Livingstone gave an admirable summary of his view of the expedition's purpose:

The main objects of the Expedition to which you are appointed mining geologist are to extend the knowledge already attained of the geography and mineral and agricultural resources of Eastern and Central Africa, to improve our acquaintance with the inhabitants, and to engage them to apply themselves to industrial pursuits and to the cultivation of their lands with a view to the production of raw material to be exported to England in exchange for British manufactures. And it may be hoped that by encouraging the natives to occupy themselves in the developement of the resources of their country a considerable advance may be made towards the extinction of the slave trade, as the natives will not be long in discovering that the former will eventually become a more certain source of profit than the latter.[9]

Livingstone was anxious that the white newcomers to Africa should treat the Africans with the same respect as he did: 'You are strictly enjoined to exercise the greatest forbearance towards the people . . . even the *appearance* of over-reaching or insulting must be carefully avoided.'[10] To John Kirk he said that tribal chiefs and the leading men of the villages ought always to be treated with great respect and nothing should be done to weaken their authority.[11]

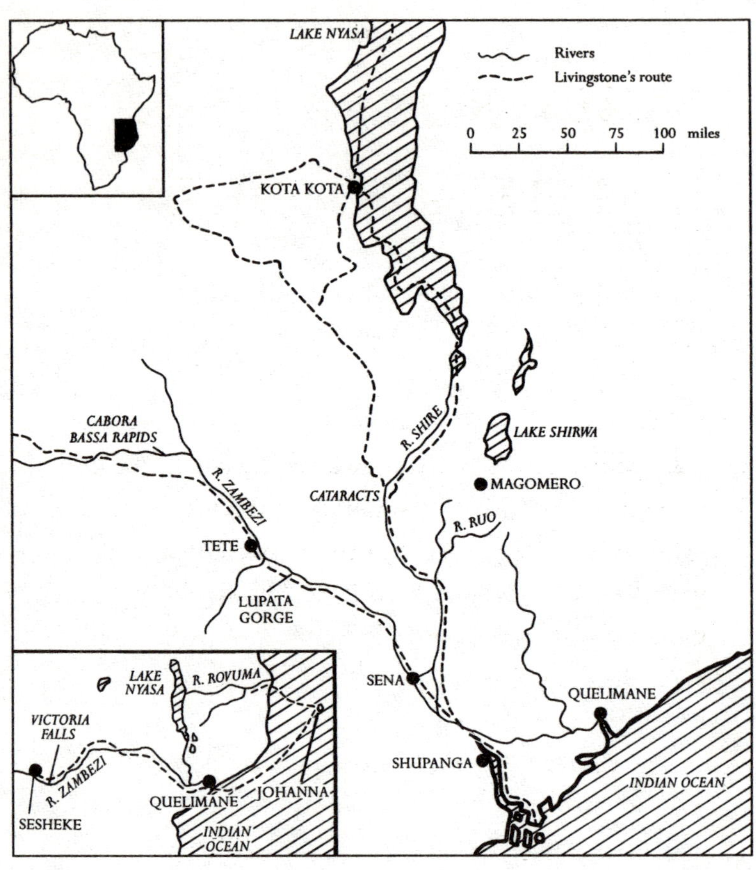

The Zambezi Expedition

MA ROBERT ON THE ZAMBEZI

*A Mission without difficulties would to me be like a man
without a shadow*[1]

The Tswana peoples address women as the mother of
their child; Mary Livingstone was therefore known
to them as Ma Robert, the mother of Robert, her eldest
child. When Livingstone named his steamboat after his
wife, he called the vessel *Ma Robert*. It was divided into
three parts to be transported by the *Pearl*, which sailed
from Birkenhead on 10 March 1858, and encountered
fierce storms in the Bay of Biscay.

The real Ma Robert, Mary, was violently sick on this
part of the voyage, and when she found her nausea
continuing in calmer waters, she realized she was
pregnant again. When they reached Cape Town,
Livingstone, doubtless with relief, handed her and
young Oswell over to her parents, the Moffats; they
were in the town awaiting the arrival, on another
vessel, of the missionaries who were assigned to

establish the new LMS Barotseland mission, which Livingstone had promoted in England. Mary was to have the baby at the Kuruman mission and then travel onward to meet her husband when the infant was old enough. The child, Anna Mary, was born healthy. Her mother, probably influenced by Mrs Moffat, decided to return to Britain with her two small children, whom she placed with her husband's mother and sisters at Hamilton, with instructions for Oswell's schooling. She then sailed back to Cape Town, to join David on the Zambezi. James Stewart, who idolized Livingstone and was going to the Zambezi to see whether a Free Church mission could be established there, showed solicitude towards her on the voyage, a care that was misinterpreted, causing a scandal. He claimed that Mary drank alcohol to excess, but we only have his word for this. We know that she used brandy and water as a cure for seasickness.

Meanwhile Livingstone had arrived at the mouth of the Zambezi. The original plan was to sail the *Pearl* upriver to Tete, offload and reconstruct the *Ma Robert*, continue on the latter vessel to Zumbo, and then march overland to Barotseland, where a prefabricated house they had brought would be erected. The LMS missionaries would then arrive overland from the Cape and Mary and the two youngest children would join them.

In the event, almost everything went wrong. It took a while to find a passage through the Zambezi delta, the captain of the *Pearl* discovered that the river was too shallow for his vessel and had to leave the party forty miles upriver, and Livingstone and his brother Charles quarrelled and came to blows. Livingstone had only the steam launch *Ma Robert*, which had been assembled in three days, a pinnace and two whaling boats in which to transport to Tete all his stores, which had filled the *Pearl*. The most severe problem was the fuelling of the *Ma Robert*. A whole day was required to cut enough wood for another day's steaming. The boat was also underpowered for the strong Zambezi current, and the steel hull soon began to rust in the humidity. Bedingfeld, in charge of the boat, proved to be such a trouble-maker that Livingstone dismissed him. Three miles above Shiramba Livingstone found a hollow and very wide baobab, inside which he cut his monogram on the bark. In 1958, when this was found, the government of Mozambique declared the baobab a historical monument.

There were also diplomatic difficulties. The Portuguese had always been concerned about Livingstone establishing posts in the interior; the Governor-General of Mozambique was told

to take, with the utmost discretion, every possible measure to find out what the plans of Dr Livingstone may be and to prevent him carrying out the suspected scheme or any others which he may attempt to put into execution without the previous consent of His Majesty's Government, so that he may not under cover of the Gospel or of Science, change his status of explorer for that of conquerer.[2]

In 1858 the Portuguese also tried to forestall him by proclaiming the land from Zumbo to the coast as the province of Zambezia, which they said belonged to them. In part of this territory they were engaged in a struggle with an Afro-Portuguese group led by Mariano and his brother Bonga. Livingstone interfered in the altercation by inviting Bonga to dine on the *Ma Robert*, an action which greatly displeased Lord John Russell, who had replaced Clarendon as British Foreign Secretary. Prince Albert, a cousin of the King of Portugal, refused an invitation to be patron of the Universities' Mission to Central Africa.

The steam launch reached Tete on 8 September 1858. The Kololo porters Livingstone had left there when he travelled downstream were delighted to see him, expecting him now to return them to their homes in Barotseland. Of 114 Kololo, 78 had survived his absence. Their repatriation was to be far from simple. Livingstone had left the course of the Zambezi when he had journeyed coastwards, missing the Cabora Bassa rapids and the Kariba gorge, both of them hazards which made the river unnavigable. On 10 November the party reached Cabora Bassa, to be faced by a waterfall of thirty feet. A reconnaissance on foot discovered further rapids. This was as far as the *Ma Robert* could steam up the Zambezi.

Livingstone abandoned in cavalier fashion the idea of going to Barotseland, turning his attention to the River Shire (pronounced 'Sheeray'), which joined the Zambezi at Sena, east of Tete, a hundred miles from the coast. His was not a personality to accept defeat or admit error. As a damage limitation exercise he would forget his extravagant claims about the Zambezi as an easy route to the interior, and explore the Shire, which flowed, according to the local people and the Portuguese, from a large lake. Livingstone had heard about this when he was in Tete in 1856, from Candido Cardoso, who had visited the lake and showed him a map of the region. Perhaps there Livingstone would find the highland plateau necessary for a mission station and trading post, and by mapping the area he could earn further acclaim as an explorer.

Leaving Rae, Baines and Thornton at Tete, Livingstone set off up the Shire in the *Ma Robert* with his brother Charles, Kirk, and Walker and Rowe, two Royal Navy men sent to replace Bedingfeld. All went well for two hundred miles, until they encountered cataracts.

They returned to Tete, to equip an expedition which would travel the first part of the journey by boat and then proceed on foot. Arriving back at the cataracts at the end of August 1859, the expedition hurried onwards on foot, reaching Lake Nyasa (now Lake Malawi) on 17 September. The haste was due to Livingstone's receipt of a letter informing him that Albrecht Roscher, a German geographer, had left Zanzibar for Lake Nyasa in search of the source of the Nile, and that Richard Burton, on the same quest, had discovered Lake Tanganyika. He displayed an unchristian anxiety that his rival should not 'discover' Lake Nyasa before him, ignoring the fact that he was not the first European to see the lake – that honour belonged to the Portuguese, for whom Livingstone had no respect. In fact, he reached the lake two months before the German (who was murdered on the way back), although he did not know this. Even though the Portuguese had preceded him, Livingstone was the first person to map and describe the area accurately.

There were other coastal visitors at Lake Nyasa: Arabs (although most of them were more accurately described as Swahilis, the word Arab will be used in this book, because that is how they were known in the nineteenth century) from Zanzibar and other seaports, who were well established in the region, having two dhows which sailed on the lake, transporting slaves from the Katanga region of present-day Zaire. The slave trade was flourishing around the lake, with slaves being taken overland to the coast for sale. 'I feel with Palmerston [the Prime Minister]', Livingstone said, 'that the slave trade must be put down before lawful commerce can succeed.'[3] On the way to the sea the slaves were used as porters of ivory. Livingstone thought that if other means could be employed to get the ivory to the coast, the slave trade would die out. He was convinced by the doctrine of the anti-slaver Fowell Buxton that legitimate trade, by its very morality, would bring an end to illegitimate trade. This was a misconception, for slaves were still greatly in demand at the coastal ports for transshipment to Arabia in the north. Even the Portuguese were still trading in slaves, despite pressure from Britain, and their captives were destined for Brazil, via the Cape of Good Hope.

Livingstone wrote to the Foreign Secretary, advocating the establishment of a British colony in the area, to repress the slave trade, for, as long as the Portuguese were in the area, he believed that slavery would not end. Earl Russell sent him a firm refusal after Palmerston had added marginalia to Livingstone's letter: 'I am very unwilling to embark on new schemes of British possessions. Dr L . . . must not be allowed to tempt us to form colonies only to be reached by forcing steamers up cataracts.'[4] However, by then Livingstone had ordered two more steamers from Britain, one to ply between Tete and the coast and the other to steam up the River Shire, to be taken apart at the cataracts and transported to Lake Nyasa, where it would trade.

A hopeless commander of Europeans, Livingstone then dismissed Baines, his talented artist, and Thornton, the geologist. Baines, who had been accused of stealing butter and sugar, went to Cape Town and joined other trader-explorers. Thornton went to Zanzibar and joined Baron von der Decken's expedition to Mount Kilimanjaro. All the white men associated with Livingstone on the Zambezi expedition came to regard him as impossible to work with and unable to be trusted. When his own interests were at stake, they felt he behaved dishonestly. He failed to consult them or explain his plans, which they frequently thought were stupid and dangerous. 'He is one of those sanguine enthusiasts wrapped up in their schemes whose reason and better judgment is blinded by headstrong passion.'[5]

Livingstone, awaiting his new steamers, decided finally to return the Kololo to Barotseland. Some had settled well at Tete and did not wish to return. But in the middle of May 1860 Livingstone, Charles, Kirk, and some of the Kololo left Tete for Barotseland, on a round trip estimated to take six months.

On the journey, they met the first white tourist at Victoria Falls and heard of the tragedy of the

Barotseland mission from the mouth of Sekeletu, a Kololo chief. The mission party, composed of Holloway Helmore, his wife and four young children, and Roger Price, his wife and baby, had travelled overland by ox wagon from Kuruman to Linyanti, which they reached in April 1860 and where they expected Livingstone to be waiting for them. He, of course, had been delayed by the unnavigable Zambezi. Both the Helmores, two of their children, Mrs Price and her baby all died of malaria a few hundred yards from the wagon Livingstone had left in Linyanti, containing his medicines, including quinine. Roger Price and the two surviving Helmore children went back to Kuruman. Livingstone missed them by six weeks. He blamed the failure of the mission on the LMS, castigating them for not having provided medical assistance, seemingly untouched by the tragedy and his own part in it. He had not been truthful about the dangers of malarial fever when he had advocated establishing a mission in Barotseland. The LMS justifiably blamed Livingstone for the whole unhappy affair. Relations between the society and their former missionary remained sour. As for Price, he became Livingstone's brother-in-law by marrying Mary's sister, Bessie Moffat. He was later to help found LMS missions on Lake Tanganyika.

On the return to Tete Livingstone decided to descend the Cabora Bassa rapids in canoes. In the inevitable overturning of the boats Kirk lost eight books of research notes on his last two years' work. Boatless, the travellers continued on foot, but did not keep together. Charles forged on ahead, leaving his brother and Kirk without food; they nearly died.

At Tete were letters telling them that a paddle steamer, the *Pioneer*, was on its way with new missionaries from the Universities' Mission to Central Africa, who would build a mission on the Shire. The *Ma Robert*, which had accomplished so much, finally sank near Sena, when its rusted hull disintegrated on hitting a sandbank.

Livingstone went to meet the *Pioneer* and the UMCA missionaries, led by Bishop Charles Frederick Mackenzie. After a diversion to see whether the highlands of the upper Shire could be reached by the Rovuma river (Livingstone was desperate for a way inland not dominated by the Portuguese), the expedition used the Zambezi route, arriving at the cataracts on 8 July 1861. A week later they came across a slave caravan, whose Yao leaders fled. Eighty-four slaves were freed. Mackenzie, wanting to talk to the Yao to dissuade them from slave-raiding, approached a village with Livingstone and the freed slaves. The Yao then launched an attack so dangerous that Livingstone gave the order to fire and himself fired a gun. This was the first time he had had to do this, for he believed that

David Livingstone in his consular dress, *c*. 1852 (by courtesy of David Livingstone Centre, Blantyre).

Livingstone's wife Mary, wearing a cameo of her husband, *c.* 1859–61 (by courtesy of David Livingstone Centre, Blantyre).

The steamboat the *Ma Robert* on the Zambezi, watercolour by Thomas Baines, 24 May 1858 (Royal Geographical Society, London).

Livingstone's letter of 29
April 1862 to his mother,
Agnes, reporting Mary's
death (Trustees of the
National Library of
Scotland).

Mary Livingstone's grave at Shupanga, photographed by John Kirk, 1862 (Trustees of the
National Library of Scotland).

Abdullah Susi, 1874 (Royal Geographical Society, London).

James Chuma (by courtesy of David Livingstone Centre, Blantyre).

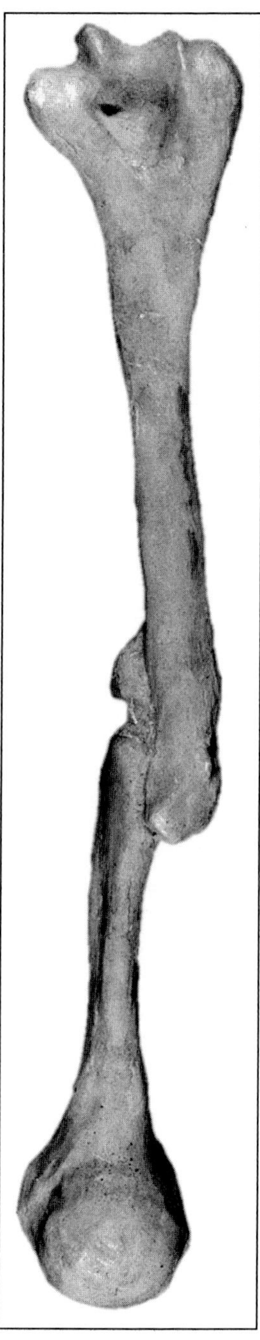

Stanley's helmet (Royal Geographical Society).

Livingstone's distinctive cap. He had these made for
him at Starkey's of Bond Street, and they became
important to his public image (Royal Geographical
Society).

Plaster cast of Livingstone's left humerus, taken from
his corpse when it reached England, 1874 (by kind
permission of the President and Council of the Royal
College of Surgeons of England).

The Livingstone family, *c.* 1856–7 (by courtesy of David Livingstone Centre, Blantyre).

Henry Morton Stanley and Kalulu, his personal servant (given to him by a slave trader when Kalulu was aged eight), who drowned crossing the Congo on Stanley's 1874–7 expedition (by courtesy of the National Portrait Gallery, London).

Jacob Wainwright with Livingstone's coffin and effects on board the vessel taking them to England, 1874 (by kind permission of Quentin Keynes).

it was a mistake to become involved in the politics and rivalries of the African tribes among whom he travelled. His view was that he was passing through their lands at their goodwill, which should not be compromised. Mackenzie, however, failed to heed this advice, and became involved in an expedition to free the captive husbands of some women. In the process he lost his medicines, which was to prove fatal. Within a short while he died from malaria.

On returning to the cataracts, Livingstone heard that Mary and the UMCA missionaries' wives were on their way from Cape Town, on a ship which also carried the second steam vessel, the *Lady Nyassa*, in pieces. He went to the mouth of the Zambezi to meet the wife he had not seen for three years and nine months, to find her feverish. He wanted to move her and two other women upriver to higher and less malarial ground as soon as possible, but was hindered by the *Pioneer* hitting sandbanks because she was laden down with the unconstructed *Lady Nyassa*. News then came to Livingstone that Mackenzie was dead. Two of his missionary colleagues were also to perish.

Mary was showing little improvement. She seemed to have lost her Christian faith, and, very depressed, she reproached her husband for his neglect of his family. By the time the Livingstones reached Shupanga, Mary was seriously ill with malaria, as well as having a yellow skin.

She was taken off the *Pioneer* to a house on shore, where she died at seven in the evening on 27 April 1862. Rae made a coffin, in which she was buried the following day beneath a large baobab tree. Her large, well-kept grave can still be seen in a walled cemetery at Shupanga.

Livingstone was distraught, for he had come to love his wife. 'Oh my Mary, my Mary! How often we have longed for a quiet home.'[6] He must have felt guilt at his treatment of her, and he poured out his misery in a stream of letters. Now in sole charge of his children, he arranged for Robert to come and join him, surely an irresponsible act in view of the conditions which had proved fatal to his wife. Robert reached the Cape, but then took a ship to New York. He joined the Northern forces in the American Civil War, was wounded in battle at Laurel Hill, and died on 5 December 1864, at the age of eighteen, in a Confederate prisoner-of-war camp in Salisbury, North Carolina. He and his father are commemorated in Livingstone College, Salisbury.

After Mary died, Livingstone pressed on with getting the *Lady Nyassa* to Lake Nyasa. The only solution seemed to be to build a road around the cataracts. While this was being constructed, on 2 July 1863 a message came from the British government: Livingstone's expedition was recalled. Since the river was too low to take the *Pioneer* to the coast, Livingstone determined to await the rains by travelling overland to the northern end of Lake

Nyasa. It was to be a journey of 750 miles, which was useful in demonstrating how the slave trade worked. Then Livingstone returned to the coast and took ship for England. The UMCA mission had also withdrawn; his failure seemed complete. 'I am very old and grey and face wrinkled like a gridiron.'[7] Yet, with his unshakeable faith, he still believed that 'it is God's own work and he will ensure its triumph'.[8]

TO ZANZIBAR AND BACK

We must take the bitter with the sweet in Providence[1]

His Zambezi hopes dashed, Livingstone took both his steamboats – *Pioneer* and *Lady Nyassa* – to the mouth of the Zambezi river. The *Pioneer*, which had been paid for by the British government, then went south to Cape Town. Livingstone decided to take the *Lady Nyassa*, the money for which had been put up by his friend James Young, to Bombay for sale in order to recoup Young's money. He and the engineer Rae took the boat under its own steam to Zanzibar, arriving on 24 April 1864. There Rae, terrified of the proposed voyage, left Livingstone. Ever resourceful, Livingstone gathered a twelve-man crew, which included Chuma and Wakatini,[2] freed slave boys he had brought with him from the Shire river, and Susi and Amoda,[3] adults who had been employed at Shupanga. The journey of 2,500 miles to Bombay was undertaken by this party, with Livingstone as navigator. His lessons in navigation from the captain of the original ship which bore him to South Africa and the astronomer royal in Cape Town stood him in magnificent stead. This sea voyage must rank as one of Livingstone's bravest feats. The boat, designed for rivers rather than oceans, arrived in Bombay on 13 June 1864, having left Zanzibar on 30 April. 'The vessel was so small that no one noticed our arrival.'[4] It was eventually sold and the money deposited in the Agra Bank, which failed. The dangerous voyage had been for nothing.

Livingstone put Chuma and Wakatini in the Free Church of Scotland mission school, and found jobs for Susi and Amoda in the Bombay docks. The Governor of Bombay, Sir Bartle Frere, invited Livingstone to be his guest. After a week at a hill station, Livingstone borrowed money for his fare to England. He arrived at Charing Cross station, London, on 23 July 1864, and took a room for himself in a hotel.

His reception was very different from that he had received in 1856. *The Times* had said he was 'unquestionably a traveller of talents, enterprise and excellent constitution, but it is now plain that his zeal and imagination much surpass his judgement'.[5] None of his aims had been achieved. The Barotseland mission had ended in disaster, the Zambezi had not proved to be navigable, the UMCA mission had had to withdraw to Zanzibar, the steamers designed to introduce legitimate commerce to counter the slave trade had been unable to reach their destination, and he had failed to establish a home with his wife, who had died in the attempt to do so. Livingstone was anxious to see his children again, but first he wrote to Murchison, still president of the Royal Geographical Society, and went to see Palmerston, the Prime Minister, and Earl Russell, head of the Foreign Office. Palmerston was civil, but Russell cold – hardly surprising after the trail of corpses Livingstone had left behind him in Africa. Livingstone was offered numerous invitations to speak in public, but he declined all except one, that to address the British Association for the Advancement of Science.

Before that meeting was due, he went to Hamilton to see his family. He had never met his youngest child, Anna Mary, now five years old. Robert, the eldest, was in America; Agnes, eighteen, lived with her aunts and grandmother, and Thomas and Oswell were at Gilbertsfield school, near Hamilton. David's mother was eighty and did not always recognize him. The cottage was too small for the literary exercise which Livingstone now had in mind. John Murray, the publisher of his previous book, was asked to find a place near London, to which Livingstone would move, with Agnes as housekeeper, in order to write a book. At this point came an invitation from Frederick Webb, who had accompanied Livingstone on one of his earliest journeys through the Kalahari. The Webbs lived at Newstead

Abbey, Nottinghamshire. They would be happy to have their old friend to stay, he was welcome to bring Agnes, and the boys could come too in their school holidays. Livingstone accepted with pleasure.

Livingstone was not the main speaker at the British Association meeting in Bath. That honour belonged to Richard Burton, who was to debate with John Hanning Speke the question of the source of the Nile. Burton and Speke had travelled together from Zanzibar to Lake Tanganyika in 1858. On the return journey the party had split, Speke going north to a lake which he called Victoria. Speke claimed that the Nile rose in Lake Victoria, while Burton reckoned Lake Tanganyika was the source. The promised debate never took place, because Speke shot himself the day before the meeting; whether accidentally or not has never been established.

Livingstone attended Speke's funeral on 23 September 1864; the whole matter whetted his appetite for finding the true source of the Nile. Speke had revisited Lake Victoria with James Augustus Grant in 1862 and found an outlet on its northern shore which reinforced his point. Samuel White Baker had also entered the controversy by discovering an alternative source, which he called Lake Albert, 150 miles north-west of Lake Victoria, which had a river flowing out of its northern section. Livingstone began to wonder whether this chain of central African lakes might be connected by rivers, in which case the source of the Nile would lie further south than Lake Tanganyika.

In January 1865 Murchison asked Livingstone whether he would go to Africa to settle the matter and discover the watershed, or watersheds, in south-central Africa from which the Nile might flow. The area south of Lake Tanganyika could be his starting point. Livingstone accepted the invitation not only to further geographical knowledge, but also, and this was most important to him, to defeat slavery. Without the ending of the slave trade in the African interior, he felt that no 'civilizing' influences or settlement had a chance of being accepted in the war-ravaged regions. Livingstone had learned his lesson with the UMCA mission to the Shire river, which had been destroyed not only by illness but also by the local wars and rivalries which stemmed from slave raiding and trading.

With the matter of his further employment settled, Livingstone settled down at Newstead Abbey to enjoy the company of his elder daughter and write his book. Before Charles had left him on the Zambezi the brothers had talked of amalgamating the journals they had each been keeping. It was Livingstone's habit to carry in his jacket pocket a little, stiff-covered book in which he made notes, sketches and rough maps. At a suitable opportunity, these jottings were elaborated and written into large, strongly bound volumes. Charles sent his work from America, and David began to merge this with his own. He complained that the work of amalgamation was a nuisance, but Agnes and Mrs Webb helped with the copying. Charles crossed the Atlantic and he and Kirk came to stay at Newstead. Mornings were filled with writing, and the afternoons were spent wandering around the estate or fishing. Agnes was instructed in social graces by Mrs Webb, who arranged for her to go to balls. Within two months of going to Newstead Livingstone was sending copy to John Murray to be set. William Cotton Oswell, the hunter he had taken through the Kalahari and who had thereafter remained his friend and correspondent, did much of the proof-reading at his home in Tunbridge Wells.

The final book, which Livingstone finished on 16 April 1865, came to 200,000 words, never mentioned Baines or Bedingfeld, and had as its constant theme the iniquities of the Portuguese. Murray printed 10,000 copies of D. and C. Livingstones' *Narrative of an Expedition to the Zambesi and its Tributaries and of the Discovery of Lakes Shirwa and Nyassa 1858–1864*, all of which were sold. The book went into five editions.

On 25 April 1865 Livingstone and Agnes left Newstead for London. The pair went sightseeing, before visiting W.C. Oswell in Tunbridge Wells and then travelling to Hamilton to be with the family. Livingstone stayed in Scotland for several weeks, during which his mother died. He was concerned about his son Tom, who was not strong. Livingstone wondered whether to take him to India, but he found work in Egypt. Anna Mary was to be sent to a Quaker school in Kendal, near Livingstone's friends the Braithwaites, Oswell was to complete his schooling (he later went on to study medicine) and Agnes was to be accompanied to Paris by her father, where she would be left in a finishing school.

Back in London, Livingstone planned for his new African expedition. He was worried about money. The Royal Geographical Society put up only £500 (Livingstone said 'I have not agreed to follow Sir Roderick entirely, but will take the matter again into consideration on the coast'[6]), Livingstone himself contributed £800 and Earl Russell at the Foreign Office offered £500, on condition that he accepted a consulship; unless he settled in one place it was not to be thought of as a salary, and he was not to enter Portuguese territories. How could he discover the sources of the Nile while sitting in one place? None the less, Livingstone accepted the offer and was appointed consul to the 'Territories of the African Kings and Chiefs in the Interior of Africa'. James Young, who had bought Livingstone the *Lady Nyassa*, gave £1,000, and there was now enough for a small expedition.

Livingstone accompanied Agnes to Paris, took the train to Marseille, and embarked on a P&O liner to

Suez. Another boat took him to Bombay (the Suez canal would not be open for another three years), where he arrived on 11 September 1865. He was again the guest of Sir Bartle Frere, the governor, who gave him twelve Indian sepoys (military men, in this case marines) as porters, and suggested he also find recruits at the government-run school for freed slaves at Nasik. He obtained nine Africans there and completed his numbers by taking Chuma and Wakatini from the school in which he had placed them, and finding Susi and Amoda at the docks. As African buffaloes, which were too fierce to be tamed, were immune to disease following bites from tsetse flies, Livingstone bought eleven Indian buffaloes as pack animals, hoping they would be similarly resistant.

In early January 1866 the little expedition sailed for Zanzibar. When they arrived ten men from the Comoro Islands joined them and final arrangements were made during a six-week sojourn on the island. On 19 March 1866 Livingstone and his party sailed for the mouth of the Rovuma river, and they disembarked on the coast of mainland Africa on 21 March. The explorer's plan was to travel up the Rovuma valley to the east of Lake Nyasa, go north to Lake Tanganyika, and see what rivers exited from its northern shore. He would thus avoid regions claimed by the Portuguese; rather, he would be in territory in which Arab slavers from Zanzibar and Kilwa, a coastal slaving town, operated. The Arab Sultan of Zanzibar had some authority over the East African littoral towns from Mogadishu in the north to the Rovuma river in the south, and some towns on the slave routes in the interior could also be said to be under his influence. He had given Livingstone a letter ordering all Arabs in the interior to assist him.

Livingstone set off for the interior with a motley group of people and even stranger animals: six camels, a donkey, two mules, three buffaloes (the rest had died) and a calf. His purpose was to discover which animals could survive the tsetse fly. In the event none of them did, although their deaths could also be attributed to ill-treatment, particularly by the sepoys, who blamed one buffalo's death on its having been attacked by a tiger. There are no tigers in Africa.

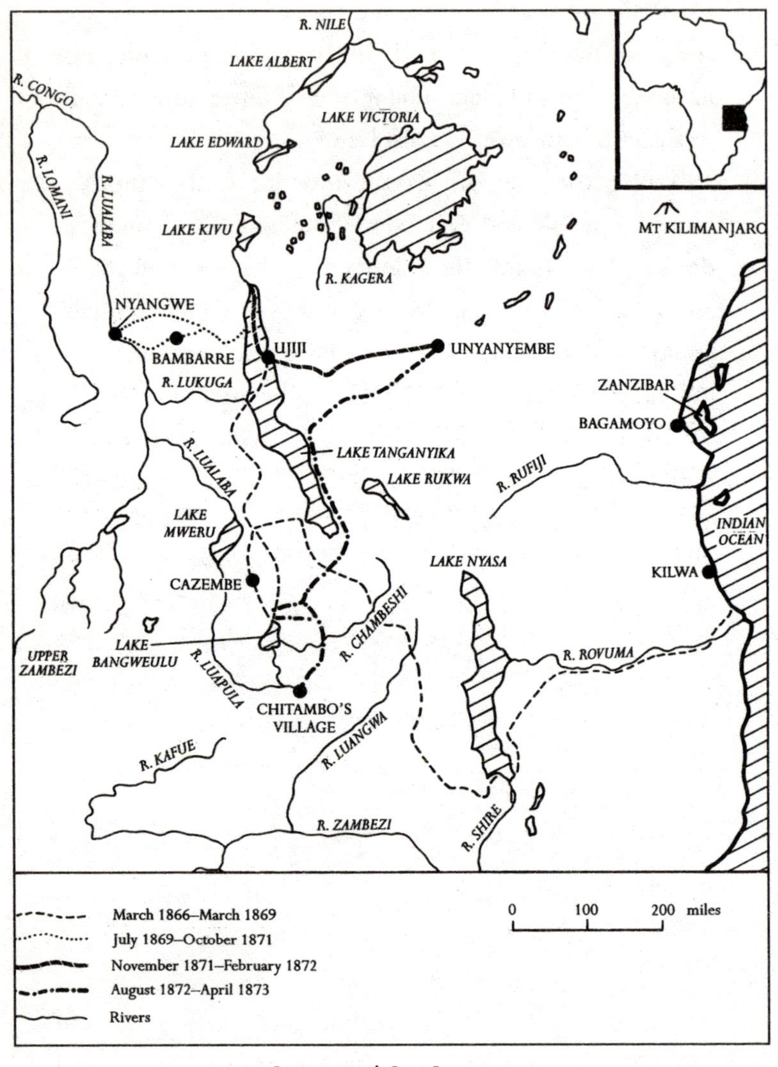

Livingstone's Last Journeys

IN THE MIDST OF THE SLAVE TRADE

Difficulties . . . what are they for but to be surmounted?[1]

Livingstone encountered three major problems as he set off inland up the valley of the Rovuma river: the terrain was forested and so impenetrable that a passage had to be hacked through by men hired locally; the animals weakened and died one by one, because of tsetse fly and possibly in the care of the camels, shock at being expected to trek through tropical jungle; and the porters hired in Bombay and Zanzibar proved to be unwilling and unsuitable. The Indian Army sepoys regarded it as unmanly to bear burdens, which became ever heavier as the animals perished, and the Nasik young men were, according to Livingstone, dishonest, unreliable and lazy. In contrast to other Europeans who were now leading porters into the African interior, Livingstone was easy-going and no disciplinarian. He had always treated the black people under his command with tolerance and humanity, and this method had worked well on his previous journeys. He liked the teenagers Chuma, a sharp lad, and Wakatini, who insisted on wearing, Arab-fashion, a nightshirt Livingstone had given him and was an incorrigible giggler, smoker and singer of 'Dididey dididey or weeweewee'.[2] Other than these two, however, he had with him a group of people who saw his tolerance as weakness and exploited it.

The difficulties were exacerbated when the party left the Rovuma valley and entered the plains, recently devastated by the Ngoni people and therefore barren. The twenty men Livingstone had hired on the coast decided to go home.

On 3 July 1866 the party reached the village ruled by Mtarika, a chief of the Yao people. The Yao were being harassed by the Ngoni, who were raiding them for slaves. Indeed, Livingstone was now on the slave route from Lake Nyasa to the coast. Whereas he had originally intended to turn north towards Lake Tanganyika from this southern route, he changed his plans on the advice of Mtarika, who informed him of dangers from the Ngoni, and decided to travel directly to Lake Nyasa, cross it by boat, and then turn northwards to approach Lake Tanganyika on the western side. Murchison, of course, had wanted him to go straight to the north of Lake Tanganyika, to see whether it was joined to Lake Victoria and thus was the source of the Nile.

Livingstone, however, thought lakes Nyasa and Tanganyika might be joined, which would push the Nile's source even further southward. He was also interested in how the two lakes west of Lake Nyasa, lakes Bangweulu and Mweru, which he had come across on his journey to the west coast of Africa in 1854, fitted into the system of waterways.

Livingstone encountered so much evidence of the slave trade on this journey that he was shocked and troubled. He must have realized that the prestige which would follow the discovery of the Nile's sources would focus public opinion on the problem of slavery in Africa. Along the way he saw corpses whose necks were enclosed by slave yokes, half-eaten by hyenas, and weak people who had been abandoned by the slave caravans, lying by the wayside. A week after he left Mtarika he met a caravan led by Sef Rubia and bound for Kilwa, the second largest slave entrepot on the coast after Zanzibar. He was offered an ox and a bag of meal, which he was reluctant to accept from one engaged in so evil a trade, but he was too hungry to resist. Thus began Livingstone's relations with the Arabs in the interior, a group he had hitherto wished to avoid.

Sef Rubia showed the party the way to the village of Mataka, another Yao chief, and then proceeded on his way to the coast, carrying letters from Livingstone, which were duly delivered to the British consul in

Zanzibar. Leaving Mataka, Livingstone arrived on the eastern shore of Lake Nyasa on 8 August 1866; he was exhilarated at his return 'to an old home I had never expected to see again . . . to bathe in the delicious waters . . . and dash in the rollers'.[3] But when he tried to hire or buy a boat to take his party, which now numbered only twenty-four, across the water, he found himself blocked at every turn. Since he was directly on the Arab slave route, the Kilwa merchants may have regarded him as a British spy and feared his reports of the slave trade would reach the British consul in Zanzibar, as indeed they were about to do in the despatches carried by Sef Rubia. Livingstone had no alternative but to go round the lake, and he headed northwards. Finding this route impassable, he turned southwards, to go round the southern shore of the lake. On the journey he travelled along a route littered with human skulls and bones.

On 13 September he saw the River Shire, which reminded him of his wife lying on the banks of the Zambezi, and Bishop Mackenzie buried nearby. Here Wakatini, the freed slave from the Nasik school in Bombay, found his home village and left Livingstone, to be replaced as his personal servant by Chuma. Soon afterwards others left, leaving Livingstone with Chuma, Susi, Amoda and the young men from Nasik. When Musa and the other Comorans reached Zanzibar, in order to receive their pay they claimed that Livingstone had died in the interior. The news reached England, but was not wholly believed, and the first of the search parties to settle the matter was organized. Lieutenant E.D. Young, formerly of Livingstone's Zambezi steamboat *Pioneer*, was appointed to lead it, and he sailed in the *Search* up the Zambezi and Shire rivers to the cataracts, which he reached on 19 August 1867. His boat was constructed in sections small enough to be carried around the cataracts (much had been learned from Livingstone's pioneering work), and the search party reached Lake Nyasa, where they learned that their quarry had rounded the south of the lake. Evidence of his presence, such as tales of his poodle Chitane and a razor he had traded, was found. Young, who had known Musa on the Zambezi, had proved that the man was lying.

By now Livingstone had travelled further. After rounding the southern shore of Lake Nyasa, he headed north-west to the Luangwa river, across a valley and up an escarpment, the summit of which was reached on Christmas Day. Livingstone felt he was now at the central African watershed, with lakes Bangweulu and Mweru to the north-west. He was in country inhabited by the Bisa people and their chief, Chitambo. It was here that several years later he was to return for his final days.

Livingstone was now at the Chambeshi river (the words Chambeshi and Zambezi are Bantu variants meaning 'great water'), which he thought might flow into Lake Bangweulu, from which the northward-flowing Luapula exited; he considered this might be a Nile source. He crossed the Chambeshi basin in the rainy season, when it was very swampy. One of the porters slipped and fell; unfortunately he was carrying the chronometer, which, unknown to Livingstone, was damaged and thereafter misplaced all readings by 20 miles to the east. In the swamp Chitane, the leader's pet poodle, disappeared, causing him to suffer a sense of grievous loss. But a disaster far more serious occurred — two Yao porters deserted, taking with them the medicine chest. Livingstone thus had no quinine to combat malaria; he felt that this was his sentence of death. Yet the swamps eventually came to an end and the party arrived at a village headed by Chitimukulu Chitapangwa, a chief of the Bemba people. Like many other peoples, the Bemba engaged in slave raiding and trading, and a Zanzibar caravan was in the village when Livingstone arrived. He took the opportunity to send letters to Zanzibar, requesting that more medicines be sent to Ujiji, on the east coast of Lake Tanganyika. When the letters arrived, they gave the lie to Musa's claim that Livingstone was dead.

Livingstone also decided to postpone his geographical research for the present and go to Ujiji himself to get medicines which should be there awaiting his arrival, having been despatched when he set out from Zanzibar in 1866. Despite having rested for three weeks at Chitapangwa's and been given ivory (as currency) and provisions by him for the onward journey, Livingstone became ill. His chest was very painful and his hearing affected. He also suffered a debilitating attack by *siafu*, often known as soldier, safari, or driver ants. After he reached the western shore of Lake Tanganyika he collapsed, and there is a month's gap in his journal, which he resumed on 30 April 1867. The place he found himself in he described as one of unsurpassed loveliness, and indeed it is now a Zambian national park.

Livingstone planned to go north along the western shore of the lake, in order to reach a place from which he could cross to Ujiji on the eastern shore, to collect his medicines. He found the way blocked by a war being waged by Tippu Tip, a Zanzibari merchant and slave and ivory trader, who was carving out for himself in the area a hegemony upheld by firearms. Livingstone was forced to stay where he was for three months, assisted by another Zanzibari merchant, Hamis, who gave him food and shelter. During this lull in his activity there was an earthquake which further damaged his chronometer, enhancing its inaccuracy by another 50 miles, to make it 70 miles out of true, although its owner remained unaware of this.

Perhaps the kindness of Hamis, and the conclusion of Tippu Tip's war, made Livingstone now decide to travel west with Tippu, rather than continue to Ujiji. In times past he would not have dreamed of accompanying or co-operating with Arab traders involved in the slave trade, but he was alone in the middle of Africa, with very few companions and no medicine, and he had been dangerously ill. He also wanted to investigate Lake Mweru and its potential as a Nile source. Tippu's version of events is thus:

Some of my men went out searching for the enemy and came across a large [in fact, he was of medium height] white man, an Englishman, whose name was Livingstone, with the first name David. . . . Some of my men brought him to camp. . . . We continued the war for two months until peace was agreed. . . . All the tusks were finished. . . . We decided to go to Kabwere near Mweru, a lake as big as Lake Tanganyika [in fact, very much smaller]. As for Livingstone, he had no goods or food. Said bin Ali and I took him. He wanted people to take him to Mweru. He went there, returned, and wanted to go to Runda Kazembe's. We gave him people to take him there and chose one of our kinsmen, Said bin Khalfan, to go as far as Kazembe's. A long time ago one of my father's relatives, Muhammed bin Saleh, had travelled as far as Kazembe's. He lost all his goods there, so stayed there. . . . We sent word to this man that Livingstone was arriving. . . . Then Livingstone needed guides to go to other places, and wherever he wanted to go he [Bin Saleh] sent him. My men returned, having left Livingstone on the borders of Runda.[4]

On 8 November Livingstone reached Lake Mweru, where he found that a large river, the Lualaba, flowed northwards from it. He made an important deduction: that the Chambeshi river flowed northwards into Lake Bangweulu, from which the Lualaba river flowed northwards to Lake Mweru, from which the Luapula flowed northwards. Could the Luapula veer eastwards into lakes Tanganyika, Victoria or Albert, and thus be a source of the Nile? In fact, it veered westwards and was a source of another great river, the Congo, although Livingstone was not to know this.

He resumed his plan to retrieve his medicines at Ujiji, and turned eastwards again to Lake Tanganyika. He was advised strongly not to go, as this was the wrong season, by Tippu Tip's relative, Muhammed bin Saleh. Impatient to be moving again, Livingstone determined to go south to Lake Bangweulu, rather than east to Ujiji. On being told of this plan, his companions united in complete rebellion; they remembered only too well the foetid swamps around Bangweulu. Livingstone managed to persuade only Susi, Chuma and three young men from Nasik (Gardner, Abraham and Simon), to accompany him. Another Arab, Muhammed bin Gharib, also joined him, and the party reached the north-western shore of the lake on 18 July 1868. Because of his broken chronometer, Livingstone placed the lake 70 miles further east than it was.

At the end of July 1868 he retraced his steps to Kazembe. Muhammed bin Gharib and a huge Arab-led caravan of slaves carrying ivory was about to set off for the south-west coast of Lake Tanganyika, and Livingstone joined it on 11 December 1868. The rainy season began again, Livingstone caught pneumonia, and on Christmas Day he collapsed. The Arabs saved his life by ordering a litter to be made for him. On this he was borne for ten weeks by slaves until they reached Maparre on the western shore of Lake Tanganyika. He was paddled across the lake to the port of Ujiji on its eastern side, and was found a hut in which to recuperate. When he sent for the goods and medicines which he expected to have been awaiting him in Ujiji, he found that most had been plundered, there was no mail, and the medicines had been left at Unyanyembe (later called Tabora), 200 miles to the east. Everyone refused to take letters from him to the east coast of Africa, 700 miles distant, for fear that he would expose the slave trade. This was to prove serious because he was in dire need of new shoes. It was not until 28 March 1869 that Livingstone was able to walk more than a few paces.

At Ujiji Livingstone heard that the Lualaba flowed north-westwards rather than to the north-east, and he felt he must ascertain whether this was true. If it was, it might be a source of the Congo instead of the Nile. His plan was now to recross Lake Tanganyika to the western shore, and travel north-westwards to the Lualaba river, which he still hoped would prove to be a western arm of the Nile. He set out with Muhammed bin Gharib, who knew that there was much cheap ivory in the region, for Manyema, to the west of Lake Tanganyika, and managed to reach Bambarre (now called Kabambare) on 21 September. Heading further west, he came to the shores of the Luama river, where he failed to find any means of crossing. He was forced to return to Bambarre on 19 December 1869. He then tried to go northwards to another part of the Lualaba, but it was the rainy season again, and he became ill, which obliged him to remain at Mamohela from 7 February to 26 June 1870. He managed to get back to Bambarre on 22 July, his only companions now Susi, Chuma and Gardner.

Livingstone was bleeding from piles, had tropical ulcers on his feet which would not heal, had intestinal bleeding and diarrhoea and was suffering from breathing problems due to his previous pneumonia. These ailments forced him to remain at Bambarre from July 1870 to February 1871, and he even allowed his chronometers to run down. His loneliness and introspection during this enforced inactivity gave rise to peculiar ideas. He convinced himself of the truth of Herodotus's theory that the Nile arose from two peaks, half of the waters flowing from which went north as the Nile, and half flowed south, and of Ptolemy's view that the Nile arose in two sources in the Mountains of the Moon, the western source passing through Lake Coloe before joining the eastern. He also read the Bible four times during his confinement, and began to believe that he might find the remains of Meroe, a city founded by Moses.

At the end of January 1871 Livingstone was cheered by the arrival at Bambarre of part of a caravan Kirk had despatched from Zanzibar in response to Livingstone's letter from Ujiji two years before. There was a letter from Kirk and some provisions and cloth. Best of all, there were quinine and seven men, who, however, maintained that Kirk had told them to bring Livingstone back to Zanzibar. This was a lie, but Livingstone believed it and bitterly criticized Kirk, who had been so loyal to him, for the rest of his life. Ignoring the views of the Zanzibar men, he prepared to try again to reach the Lualaba river. His party left Bambarre on 2 February 1871. On reaching Mamohela a few days later he received more letters, one from his daughter Agnes, and he heard that goods were awaiting him at Ujiji. He pressed on, reaching the Lualaba on 29 March at the village of Nyangwe. There he stayed for three months, unable to cross the river because no one would give him a canoe.

At Nyangwe he witnessed an appalling massacre of Africans by Arabs, in which 400 people were killed. He no longer wanted to remain in the area and retraced his steps to Bambarre, which he reached on 22 August. He then struggled, ill, on towards Lake Tanganyika, crossed it and arrived in Ujiji on 5 November. There Sherif, who had stayed at Ujiji with his supplies, told him that he had divined on the Koran, found that the doctor was dead and sold off the 3,000 yards of calico and 700 pounds of beads, altogether worth £600, which belonged to Livingstone. Livingstone was destitute and once more reliant on the Arab merchants for gifts and credit. Then, unexpectedly, on 9 November he heard that a large caravan was approaching, led by a white man.

SEVEN

A SOJOURN WITH STANLEY

A doctor ought to keep a cheerful countenance and blythe tongue[1]

The man who walked into Ujiji on 10 November 1871, at the head of a caravan of porters, was Henry Morton Stanley, a newspaper reporter attached to the *New York Herald*, who had been despatched to Africa by that journal's editor, in quest of Livingstone. He had been born out of wedlock to a woman named Rowlands and left in a Welsh workhouse. He ran away to sea at the age of fifteen, crossed to America, and was taken under the wing of a New Orleans merchant called Henry Hope Stanley, whose name he adopted.

At Zanzibar he had organized a caravan for the interior of Africa, trying to hide his intention of searching for Livingstone from the British consul, Kirk, and others. He had hired 192 porters and 2 white men, spent £4,000 on goods and stores, which included two collapsible boats, and left the coastal port of Bagamoyo for Ujiji on 22 March 1871. Both whites had died on the way, and Stanley had kept order among the bearers by whipping and threatening to shoot them. Despite this cruel regime, he arrived with fewer than fifty men.

The meeting with Livingstone is best described in Stanley's own words:

> As I advanced slowly towards him I noticed he was pale, that he looked weary and wan, that he had grey whiskers and moustache, that he wore a bluish cloth cap with a faded gold band around it, and that he had on a red-sleeved waistcoat and a pair of grey tweed trousers. I would have run to him, only I was a coward in the presence of such a mob, – would have embraced him, but that I did not know how he would receive me; so I did what moral cowardice and false pride suggested was the best thing, – walked deliberately up to him, took off my hat and said: 'Dr Livingstone, I presume?'[2]

Livingstone smiled, raised his hat and said 'Yes'. Today you can see at Ujiji a stone memorial to Livingstone on the spot where the meeting took place. Stanley brought letters from his children and plenty of nourishing food. The two men talked long into the night and over the next few weeks Stanley took personal charge of making proper meals for Livingstone, who had by now lost almost all his teeth. Gradually the sick man regained his strength, while he heard about the opening of the Suez canal, the laying of the transatlantic telegraph, and other European and American news.

The two got along well, the elder man showing the younger both sides of his character — saintly and forgiving in one mood, and resentful and vituperative about people (generally whites), whom he believed to have turned against him and betrayed him, in another. In his letters he made violent attacks on Kirk, most unjustly, although, according to Stanley, the consul had described Livingstone as a misanthrope who hated the sight of Europeans, was impossible to please and could get along with no one. Stanley decided to stay a while with the older man, who still wanted to cross the Lualaba in search of his fountains (sources of the Nile). However, Stanley told him that Murchison of the Royal Geographical Society remained interested in exploration of the northern shore of Lake Tanganyika. In mid-November they set out by boat to explore the area. On the 27th they discovered that the river exiting at the north of the lake, the Lusize, in fact flowed into, not out of, Lake Tanganyika. When Burton and Speke had seen it in 1868 they had been unable to get close enough to determine the direction of the water's flow.

This destroyed Livingstone's theory that Lake Tanganyika was the source of the Nile, or that the string of central African lakes all flowed towards the Nile. He was left with the possibility that the Lualaba was its source, and he conjectured that a river running westward out of Lake Tanganyika might join the Lualaba. He wanted to go south in search of four fountains west of Lake Bangweulu (a variation on Ptolemy's theory), before he explored the northern direction of the Lualaba. Stanley, however, thought it was time that he returned to the coast to break the news of his human, rather than geographical, discovery. The two men travelled together to Unyanyembe, where Livingstone thought there would be stores awaiting him. In vain did Stanley try to persuade Livingstone to return home, if only to get himself a set of false teeth, and to have his piles and persistent anal bleeding attended to.

At Unyanyembe Livingstone found awaiting him letters and four flannel shirts sent by his daughter Agnes. Most importantly, he also received new boots sent by Horace Waller, who had been one of Bishop Mackenzie's group on the Shire river. Livingstone had been trying out some new boots made by Seadon, which had proved most unsatisfactory – indeed, he threatened to expose Seadon before a magistrate. He had been forced to make do with 'French boots and shoes – patent leather abominations much too small for my Herculean feet'.[3] Most of the goods Kirk had sent him had been looted.

He packed up his journal, put five locks on it, wrote scores of letters, and handed the items to Stanley to take to England. He also asked Stanley to send him porters from the coast. The two men parted on 14 March 1872, Livingstone reconciling himself for a long wait at Unyanyembe until Stanley's recruits arrived. Although he liked the town, the isolation from the company of whites again led to his mind deteriorating. He became uncertain and suspicious. On 26 June he received a letter from his twenty-one-year-old son Oswell, who had written it at Bagamoyo on 14 May. Oswell, a medical student, was there with a search expedition sponsored by the RGS. When Stanley reached Bagamoyo with his news, the RGS expedition was disbanded and Oswell went home. It seems odd that he did this when he was so tantalizingly near to his father, but Stanley must have told him that Livingstone did not intend to return home yet.

At Zanzibar Stanley, with the help of £1,000 from the British government, granted so that Livingstone could continue his exploration, recruited fifty porters, who included six Nasik young men, and despatched them to Unyanyembe, where Livingstone had been waiting for five months. During that time he had heard of the death of Sir Roderick Murchison, which caused him much grief, since Murchison had been the person who had believed most deeply in Livingstone. Lord Clarendon of the Foreign Office had also died. None the less, Livingstone determined to complete the work he had set out to do, to prove that the Lualaba was a source of the Nile (though he was now uncertain about this, fearing that it might well be the Congo). This was the opinion Stanley had held, and indeed it was he who proved the theory correct four years later.

On 14 August 1872 fifty-seven men and boys, led by Chowpereh and Manua Sera,[4] arrived at Unyanyembe for Livingstone. On 25 August the explorer set out with these and the four men who had been with him so long – Chuma, Susi, Gardner and Amoda.[5] There were also two women in the party – Livingstone's cook, Halima, who was Amoda's wife, and Chuma's wife Ntaoeka. Among the six Nasik pupils were two brothers, John and Jacob Wainwright.[6] The plan was to skirt Lake Tanganyika's southern shore, proceed to Lake Bangweulu's southern shore, also skirt that, and continue west to Katanga and the four fountains or sources of the Nile. The expedition would then return to the coast and Livingstone would go back to Britain to write up his research, which would provide an income. 'I am now off and very thankful at the prospect of finishing my work.'[7]

EIGHT

LIVINGSTONE'S FINAL DAYS

It is not all pleasure, this exploration[1]

Livingstone led his party along the south-westerly route to Lake Tanganyika. Almost immediately they encountered problems, the most serious of which was that Livingstone's box of powdered milk had been left behind. He used milk as a primary source of sustenance, because of his lack of teeth, his piles and intestinal troubles. He soon developed dysentery, but continued to travel. The party arrived at Kampambwe village, to the south of Lake Tanganyika, nine weeks after they had left Unyanyembe. Livingstone determined to strike south-west to the point where the Chambeshi river entered Lake Bangweulu. He was, however, puzzled, because his measurements did not tally with those he had made in 1867, which were, of course, made on faulty chronometers, whereas he now had a new one provided by Stanley. He therefore hired guides, who led him to the lake by the beginning of January 1873.

Because of his previous false readings, Livingstone thought he was on the north-eastern edge of the lake. He must therefore turn south-eastwards to get to the lake's south side, despite the contradictory advice of his guides. He thus made a disastrous error, entering the swamps beside the lake in the rainy season. He searched this area for the Chambeshi river from mid-January, until he finally reached it on 25 March. His men carried him in relays, because the acute pain in his colon made it difficult for him to walk. His companions took him to the village of Mwela Mwape (or Kabende), belonging to Chitambo, a chief in the Ilala region, 40 miles south of Lake Bangweulu, on the banks of the Lulimala river. They built a pole and thatch hut, and laid him in it on 30 April 1873. The final entries in his journal read:

> *Apr 10th*   I am pale, bloodless and weak, from bleeding profusely ever since the 31st of March last; an artery gives off a copious stream, and takes away my strength. Oh, how I long to be permitted by the Over Power to finish my work!
>
> *Apr 18th*   Very ill all night, but remembered the bleeding and most other ailments in this land are forms of fever.
>
> *Apr 19th*   It is not all pleasure, this exploration. No observations now, owing to great weakness: I can scarcely hold a pencil, and my stick is a burden.

Apr 27th   Knocked up quite, and remain – recover – sent to buy milch goats. We are on the banks of R. Molilamo [Lulimala].[2]

Shortly before midnight on 30 April he asked Susi: 'How many days is it to the Luapula?' When told it was three days, he said 'Oh dear, dear', and then slept. An hour later he asked Susi for some water, and then said 'All right, you can go out now'. These were his last words. At 4 a.m. on 1 May, Majwara, who was on watch outside the hut, called Susi. They found Livingstone dead on his bed.

What was the cause of Livingstone's death? When his companions disembowelled him, they found what they described as a large blood clot in the region of the colon. This could have been a chronically enlarged malarial spleen, but he did not die from malaria. It is likely that the cause of death was profusely bleeding piles. Livingstone had been suffering from these haemorrhoids for years. In 1863 he reported 'Yesterday for the first time I walked a little without feeling as if I should faint. This may be the effects of the iron I have taken three times.'[3] When in Scotland in 1865 he had been strongly urged to have an operation, but had refused because 'I don't like to get my infirmities put into News papers'.[4] When Stanley had met him at Ujiji he had remarked on his paleness; he was probably anaemic.

At dawn Livingstone's followers decided to take his body to the coast, under the leadership of Susi. They removed the viscera and heart, placed them in an iron box and buried them at the foot of a large tree (Parinari curatellifola or mpundu) while Jacob Wainwright, the only literate person among them, read the funeral service. On the tree was carved Livingstone May 4 1873 Yazuza Mniasere Vchopere. The tree is dead, but the original section with the recarved inscription is preserved in the Royal Geographical Society in London. The site of the tree is today marked with an obelisk topped with a cross.[5]

They rubbed the corpse inside and out with salt, and hung it in the sun to dry, turning it every day for a fortnight. Then they bathed it in brandy, strapped the legs to the torso, wrapped it in cloth and placed it in a bark cylinder covered in cloth and waterproofed with tar. They set off with Livingstone's body, notes and instruments in mid-May, traversing 700 miles to Unyanyembe, which was reached in October. There they found a search party which had been sent to find the explorer (it had included young Robert Moffat, Robert Moffat's son, but he had died shortly after leaving Bagamoyo). Its leader, Lieutenant Verney Lovett Cameron, took Livingstone's instruments, which were never returned, and continued across Africa, leaving the corpse to be carried to Bagamoyo. Two whites from

Cameron's group accompanied it, but one of them committed suicide along the way.

Altogether seventy-nine men and women reached the coast. When they neared Bagamoyo, Chuma travelled ahead to Zanzibar, to tell Captain W.F. Prideaux, standing in for Kirk, who was on leave. Prideaux heard the news on 3 February 1874, and went to Bagamoyo to escort the body across to Zanzibar island. He opened the package in the presence of the agency doctor, confirmed the body was Livingstone's because he could recognize the features, and asked some Lazarist missionaries to construct a coffin. In this rough wooden coffin, stained black, with an inner shell of zinc, on 11 March the body, accompanied by Jacob Wainwright, was shipped to Aden on the first mailship, lying in a cabin fitted out as a mortuary chapel. It was transferred to the P&O liner *Malwa*, still watched over by Wainwright and, from Alexandria, by Livingstone's son Tom. They arrived at Southampton on 15 April 1874.

There the body was greeted by a twenty-one gun salute. As a band played Handel's *Dead March*, it was escorted to the station, where there awaited a special train to take it to London. A post mortem was performed. 'The lower limbs were so severed from the trunk that the length of the bulk of the package was reduced to a little over 4 feet.'[6] The features of the face could not be recognized by now, but there was plentiful hair on the scalp. The circumference of the cranium from the occiput to the brow was 23⅞ inches, and there was an ununited fracture in the region of the attachment of the deltoid to the humerus.

The body then lay in state for two days in the Royal Geographical Society, surrounded by palms and lilies. A plaster cast was taken of the humerus broken by a lion. A day of national mourning was announced. There was a funeral at state expense in Westminster Abbey on 18 April 1874, attended by the Prince of Wales. Before the coffin walked Livingstone's two surviving sons and their grandfather, Robert Moffat, and the pallbearers were Jacob Wainwright and Stanley in front, Horace Waller, Edward D. Young (a naval man who had been with the *Pioneer* on the Zambezi), John Kirk (who had been on the Zambezi expedition and was now consul in Zanzibar), William Cotton Oswell and William Webb (first known to Livingstone as hunters and later lifelong friends), and General Sir Thomas Steele (also a hunter who had accompanied Livingstone). Behind the coffin walked Roger Price, the survivor of the mission to the Kololo, and Kalulu, an African boy who was in Stanley's employment. A wreath from Queen Victoria was laid on the coffin. The congregation sang 'O God of Bethel', and the hundreds of hymn sheets being turned over sounded like a sigh. Canon Conway preached a sermon, saying that the last resting place into which they had lowered Livingstone was in truth his first.

On the tablet that marks the grave, which is in Westminster Abbey's nave close to that of the Unknown Warrior, are the words:

BROUGHT BY FAITHFUL HANDS

OVER LAND AND SEA

HERE RESTS

DAVID LIVINGSTONE,

MISSIONARY, TRAVELLER, PHILANTHROPIST,

BORN MARCH 19. 1813,

AT BLANTYRE, LANARKSHIRE,

DIED MAY 1. 1873,

AT CHITAMBO'S VILLAGE, ULALA.

For 30 years his life was spent in an unwearied effort to evangelize the native races, to explore the undiscovered secrets, to abolish the desolating slave trade, of central Africa, where with his last words he wrote:

> "All I can add in my solitude, is, may Heaven's
> rich blessing come down on everyone,
> American, English, or Turk, who will help
> to heal this open sore of the world."

In 1874 James Young paid for Susi and Chuma to visit England for four months, where they helped Horace Waller prepare Livingstone's last journal for publication.

They and Wainwright returned to Zanzibar. Livingstone's son Tom died in Egypt in 1876 and his son Oswell became a physician, practised in Trinidad, and died in 1892 when he was forty-one. Livingstone's daughter Agnes married in 1875 Alexander Low Bruce, director of an Edinburgh brewery, had two children and died in 1912 when she was fifty-five. His other daughter, Anna Mary, only fifteen at the time of the funeral, married a missionary, Frank Wilson, and lived until 1939. She left a son, Dr John Wilson.

NINE

CONCLUSION

He was like the rest of us, not perfect. . . . With all the honours that were heaped upon him there remained about him to the last, that which I can only call a kind of sanctified naturalness[1]

'We are only morning stars shining in the dark,' wrote Livingstone in his journal, 'but the morn will break – the good time coming yet.'[2] Livingstone saw himself as the foundation on which the house would be built, the agent of a future better world, the pathfinder. He did not regard his role as to settle and Christianize the heathen, but to forge the way for others to do so. He was the opener of Africa to others, a door through which people would enter, preach and establish legitimate trade which would supplant and therefore drive out the inhumane slave trade.

Livingstone had ecumenical tendencies from the beginning, and this tolerance extended to Africans and their traditional beliefs. He read his Bible assiduously, taught his porters hymns and preached to them in Sunday services.

As the years of Livingstone's sojourn in Africa unfolded, his views changed in subtle ways and his ideas were modified. He began as a traditional missionary at Kuruman, from where his ambition led him to establish three missions, each further removed from Kuruman. When visited in these remote places by white hunters and traders, he gladly accompanied them to regions and geographical features which he had learned about from local Africans. On such journeys the romance and excitement of being where no white man had trod before caught hold of him and impelled him to make further forays into 'the unknown'.

On his first return to Britain he was encouraged to write up and publish the notes and journals he had kept. The resultant high sales and fame in a Victorian society entranced by 'the Dark Continent' led him to explore further afield. He travelled vast distances on foot, riding a donkey or ox, or by ox wagon, developing theories about African rivers, their paths and potential. Encouraged by the Royal Geographical Society, he sloughed off his missionary bonds, although he never lost track of the fact that everything he did was for God's sake.

As he explored further, he experienced at first hand the depredations of the slave trade in the African interior. Well aware of the activities of the Anti-Slavery Society, founded in Britain in 1839, he saw his new mission partly as a moral crusade against the slave trade. His pre-missionary life in a cotton mill, together with the importance of cotton in international trade in the mid-nineteenth century, encouraged him to view the planting of cotton on highlands in Africa as a prerequisite for the establishment of legitimate trade. In one of the last letters he wrote to his daughter Agnes, he said: 'No one can estimate the amount of God-pleasing good that will be done, if by divine favour this awful slave-trade, into the midst of which I have come, be abolished. This will be something to have lived for, and the conviction has grown in my mind that it was for this end I have been detained so long.'[3]

Everywhere he went he sought suitable highlands, free from malaria and tsetse fly, where missions could be established to encourage cotton growing and trade. At times he envisaged white settlement in these regions, although before about 1857 this was not a primary aim. Rather, he wanted to encourage Africans in their own economic development. Unlike many other African explorers and missionaries, his attitude to Africans was mostly kindly and sympathetic. His exploratory progress across Africa was non-violent; there was a mutual regard and respect between himself and Africans, whom he did not see as intellectual inferiors. Later visitors to the lands of the Kololo found that the Africans remembered him for his *butu*, his sense of human kindness. He carefully documented African culture in his letters and journals.

He behaved with strict morality. Sir Harry Johnston, a later explorer who covered some of the same territory, used as porters some of the men who had been with Livingstone. Listening to them discussing scandals surrounding various explorers, he recorded: 'Dr Livingstone, who according to their traditions was sometimes cross and even peevish, who was sometimes in their eyes unreasonable and sometimes inexplicable in his actions, was nevertheless absolutely pure from the least suspicion of immorality.'[4]

Livingstone's travels have on occasion been regarded as a failure, for the Zambezi, Shire and Rovuma rivers proved to be unnavigable, the 'healthy' positions he chose for the establishment of mission stations became white men's graves, and he never discovered the source of the Nile, which he sought for so long. In fact, his journeys were a triumph. Having made astronomical and chronometrical observations for latitude and longitude, the scientific data he gathered – geographical, botanical, astronomical, ethnological, linguistic, medical, and pertaining to natural history – were copious and excellent in quality. He produced maps of the African interior more accurate than those few provided by the Portuguese. He knew about the scourge of the tsetse fly, which prevented the use of pack animals and horses, and he was adept at the use of quinine for malaria, although he remained ignorant of malaria's cause, the mosquito.

His advocacy of steamboats to foster commerce on the Zambezi and African lakes was frustrated in his own lifetime, yet three years after his death a steamboat (named the *Ilala*) was launched on Lake Nyasa, and by 1896 there were seventeen ships on the lake. His crusade against the slave trade, together with the activities of others, forced the Sultan of Zanzibar to close the slave market there. His missions were withdrawn in his lifetime, but within ten years of his death successful mission stations had been established on the south shore of Lake Nyasa, at Blantyre (named after his birthplace) at the foot of the Shire highlands, at Likoma island, halfway along the lake, at Khondowe at the northern end of the lake, on Lake Tanganyika and in Barotseland. The missionaries were closely associated with the founders of the Livingstonia Central Africa Company, which grew into the African Lakes Company.

The presence of the missionaries, whose attitude to European settlement was ambivalent, allowed Britain, having used chartered companies to secure their position, to claim protectorates and colonies after the 1884–5 Berlin Congress ushered in a period of European expansion in the African continent.

What sort of a person was this man who revealed Africa to the Europeans? The fact that he was a Scot is important, for he had imbibed in his childhood and adolescence the ideas of self-help, hard work and thrift which the Lowland Scots saw as an insurance against destitution and a means of self-improvement. Significantly, other explorers and successful missionaries came from Scotland – James Bruce, Mungo Park, Hugh Clapperton, W.B. Baikie, Robert Moffat and John Philip. There was a trait of dour stubbornness and wilful self-sacrifice in Livingstone which owed its origin to his Scottish background. His natural strong will, ambition, physical energy, dogged refusal to give up when faced with intransigent problems, and absence of self-pity when experiencing great physical discomfort and pain, created a man who would willingly undergo hardship in pursuit of his imaginative ideals. According to John Kirk, 'His absolute lack of any sense of fear amounted almost to a weakness. He would go into the most perilous positions without a tremor or a touch of hesitation.'[5]

Had he been a rationalist, he would have given up; a pragmatist, he would have abandoned his journeys; unambitious, he would not have spent his last years chasing the source of the Nile; socially adept, he would not have developed such sympathy and rapport with Africans. He was an optimistic and obsessive idealist, who achieved his aim of opening a way into Africa for others. A huge statue of Livingstone,[6] carved by the sculptor Sir W.R. Dick and unveiled in 1934, stands at Victoria Falls in Zimbabwe, facing across the Zambezi river to Zambia, where the nearby town of Livingstone lies. When Zimbabwe and Zambia finally achieved independence from their European masters, the statue was not toppled, nor the town renamed.

N O T E S

For full details of the books cited, see bibliography.

Chapter One

1.   Richard Cecil, Livingstone's tutor in the LMS seminary, to London Missionary Society, 26 January 1839, LMS archive in School of Oriental and African Studies (SOAS), London University.
2.   The tenement building at Blantyre had fallen into disrepair by 1929, when it was transformed into the Scottish National Memorial to David Livingstone. Eight miles outside Glasgow, it is well worth a visit, to see the room in which he was born and where he grew up. It has many artefacts, documents and photographs.
3.   The first instance when Livingstone added 'e' to his name occurs in a letter he wrote in Cape Town on 17 March 1852. However, he did not consistently use an 'e' until 1857.
4.   Livingstone to T.L. Prentice, 27 January 1841, Livingstone Museum, Livingstone, Zambia.
5.   Livingstone to T.L. Prentice, 5 March 1841, Livingstone Museum, Livingstone, Zambia.
6.   Livingstone to Revd William Fairbrother, 14 January 1851, Livingstone Museum, Livingstone, Zambia.
7.   Livingstone to Arthur Tidman (London Missionary Society foreign secretary), 17 March 1847, LMS archive in SOAS.
8.   Although often called his consular cap, Livingstone wore the cap many years before he became a consul. He persisted in wearing it wherever he went in Britain, despite the current fashion of top hats. He ordered the caps from the tailor Henry Drummond, of Glasgow. See J.I. Macnair, *Livingstone the Liberator*, p. 369.
9.   Livingstone to Robert Newton, 17 July 1843, in M. Boucher (ed.), *Livingstone Letters*.

10. Richard Burton, *Mission to Gelele, King of Dahomey*, 1864.

11. Livingstone to a correspondent at the Mission House, Mabotsa, 28 April 1845, in Boucher (ed.), *Livingstone Letters*.

12. Livingstone to Robert Newton, 17 July 1843, in Boucher (ed.), *Livingstone Letters*.

13. Michael Gelfand, *Livingstone the Doctor*, p. 58.

14. The final breakthrough connecting mosquitoes with malaria, for which he won the Nobel Prize, was made in 1897 by Ronald Ross (1857–1932).

CHAPTER TWO

1. Livingstone to Miss C. Ridley, 26 February 1840 (Livingstone actually meant 1841), Livingstone Museum, Livingstone, Zambia.

2. Max Gluckman, 'As Men are Everywhere Else' in B.W. Lloyd (ed.), *Livingstone 1873–1973*, p. 43.

3. Isaac Schapera (ed.), *Livingstone's African Journal* II, 243.

4. Ibid., I, 234.

5. Livingstone to Revd William Fairbrother, 14 January 1851, Livingstone Museum, Livingstone, Zambia.

6. David Livingstone, *Missionary Travels*, p. 447.

7. Ibid., p. 449. But see p. 51 for Livingstone carving his monogram inside a huge, hollow baobab.

CHAPTER THREE

1. Livingstone to Horace Waller, 6 September 1864, Waller Papers, Rhodes House, Oxford.

2. William G. Blaikie, *The Personal Life of David Livingstone*, p. 199.

3. William Monk (ed.), *David Livingstone's Cambridge Lectures*, pp. 46–7.

4. A.Z. Fraser, *Livingstone and Newstead*.

5. R.J. Campbell, *Livingstone*, p. 239, quoting J.W. Clarke, the Cambridge registrar.

6. Livingstone to Professor Adam Sedgwick, 6 February 1858, Livingstone Museum, Livingstone, Zambia.

7. Monk (ed.), *Cambridge Lectures*, p. 24.

8. Livingstone to Horace Waller, 28 April 1863, Waller Papers, Rhodes House, Oxford.

9. Livingstone to Richard Thornton, 16 April 1858, Waller Papers, Rhodes House, Oxford.

10. Ibid.

11. Livingstone to Kirk, 18 March 1858, in R. Foskett (ed.), *The Zambezi Doctors*, p. 45.

CHAPTER FOUR

1. Livingstone to Horace Waller, 2 September 1872, Waller Papers, Rhodes House, Oxford.

2. Adriano Ferreri to Governor-General of Mozambique, 31 May 1859, reproduced in M.V. Jackson Haight, *European Powers and South-East Africa*, p. 342.

3. Livingstone to Horace Waller, 28 April 1863, Waller Papers, Rhodes House, Oxford.

4. Russell to Livingstone, 2 August 1862, National Archives of Zimbabwe. See also Boucher (ed.), *Livingstone's Letters*.

5. Kirk to James Stewart in J.P.R. Wallis (ed.), *The Zambezi Journal of James Stewart*, p. 228.

6. Blaikie, *The Personal Life of David Livingstone*, p. 299.

7. Livingstone to W.C. Oswell, 15 July 1865, Waller Papers, Rhodes House, Oxford.

8. Livingstone to Horace Waller, 30 July 1862, Waller Papers, Rhodes House, Oxford.

CHAPTER FIVE

1. Livingstone to Horace Waller, 21 April 1863, Waller Papers, Rhodes House, Oxford.

2. James Chuma, born *c.* 1850, released as a slave 17 July 1861, UMCA 1861–4, to India on *Lady Nyassa*, with Livingstone's expedition 1865–74, in England 1874, later with James Thomson, died Zanzibar 1882. Wakatini [Wekotani], released as a slave July

1861, UMCA 1861–4, to India on *Lady Nyassa*, with Livingstone 1865–6, stayed at Mponda's village September 1866, assisted Livingstonia Mission, 1875–6.

3.   Abdullah (David) Susi, from Shupanga, with Livingstone 1863–4, to India on *Lady Nyassa*, with Livingstone's expedition 1866–74, name (as Yazuza or Souza) on Livingstone's tree, in England 1874, UMCA caravan leader, also with Church Missionary Society, with H.M. Stanley 1879–82, died Zanzibar 5 May 1891. Amoda (Hamoydah), from Shupanga, with Livingstone 1863–4, to India on *Lady Nyassa*, with Livingstone's expedition 1866–74, with H.M. Stanley 1874–6, died 29 January 1876 at Bwera, Buganda.

4.   D. and C. Livingstone, *Narrative of an Expedition to the Zambesi*, p. 584.

5.   *The Times*, 20 January 1863.

6.   Livingstone to Horace Waller, 2 December 1865, Waller Papers, Rhodes House, Oxford.

CHAPTER SIX

1.   Livingstone to Waller, 28 April 1863, Waller Papers, Rhodes House, Oxford.

2.   Livingstone to Waller, 3 November 1866, Waller Papers, Rhodes House, Oxford.

3.   Horace Waller (ed.), *The Last Journals of David Livingstone*, I, 90–91, entry for 8 August 1866.

4.   Maisha ya Hamed bin Muhammed el Murjebi yaani Tippu Tip, Supplement to the East African Swahili Committee Journal, 28/2, July 1958. Section given here translated by C.S. Nicholls.

CHAPTER SEVEN

1.   Livingstone to Waller, 18 August 1863, Waller Papers, Rhodes House, Oxford.

2.   H.M. Stanley, *How I Found Livingstone*, p. 331.

3.   Livingstone to Waller, 19 February 1872, Waller Papers, Rhodes House, Oxford.

4.   Chowpereh, born *c.* 1840, from Bagamoyo, with H.M. Stanley 1871–2, with Livingstone on last journey 1872–4, name (as Uchopere) on Livingstone's tree, with Stanley 1874–7 and from 1882 onwards. Manua Sera, a freed slave, with John Hanning Speke 1860–62, with Stanley 1871–2, on Livingstone's last journey 1872–4, name (as Mniasere) on Livingstone's tree, later with Stanley, James Thomson, Frederick Jackson and Count Teleki, died *c.* January 1888, of tuberculosis, at Lake Baringo.

5.   Edward Gardner, freed slave from Nasik school in Bombay, on Livingstone's last expedition 1866–74, with Stanley 1874–5, died at Camp Gardner, of typhoid fever, 14 February 1875.

6.   Jacob Wainwright, a freed slave, educated at Nasik school in Bombay; was on first Livingstone relief expedition led by Lt. Llewellyn S. Dawson; was hired by Stanley for the caravan of men and goods he despatched to Livingstone in Unyanyembe; joined Livingstone 1872; on Livingstone's last journey; cut inscription on tree; accompanied body to coast; went to England with body; with Church Missionary Society in Mombasa, Zanzibar and Buganda; died April 1892 in Urambo.

7.   Livingstone to Horace Waller, 2 September 1872, Waller Papers, Rhodes House, Oxford.

CHAPTER EIGHT

1.   Campbell, *Livingstone*, p. 328.

2.   Ibid.

3.   Livingstone to Horace Waller, 30 May 1863, Waller Papers, Rhodes House, Oxford.

4.   Livingstone to Kirk, 1 September 1864, in Foskett, *The Zambezi Doctors*, p. 80.

5.   When the tree was reported to be decaying in 1899, the lower portion was cut out so that the inscription could be preserved. It was brought to England and placed in the Royal Geographical Society's headquarters in London. A photograph of the tree in Campbell, *Livingstone*, p. 333, clearly shows one name as Souza, not

Yazuza. The inscription must have been recarved at some point, for there are photographs with Yazuza as the name. The tree was replaced by a 20 foot-tall stone obelisk in 1903.

6.   Post-mortem report by Sir William Fergusson, *British Medical Journal*, 18 April 1874.

CHAPTER NINE

1.   Stewart to Blaikie, 14 March 1881, quoted in Bridglal Pachai (ed.), *Livingstone: Man of Africa*, p. 107.

2.   Schapera (ed.), *Livingstone's African Journal*, I, 57–8 (entry for 22 January 1854).

3.   Livingstone to Agnes, 15 August 1872, in G. Seaver, *David Livingstone: His Life and Letters*, p. 610.

4.   H.H. Johnston, *Livingstone and the Exploration of Central Africa*, p. 365.

5.   Sir John Kirk interviewed by Basil Matthews, *London Missionary Society Chronicle*, December 1912.

6.   There is also a statue, unveiled in 1953, sculpted by T.B. Huxley-Jones, which can be seen from the street, on the north side of the Royal Geographical Society's building in Kensington Gore, London. *Royal Geographical Society Journal*, CXX, part 1, March 1954, pp. 15–20.

B I B L I O G R A P H Y

Blaikie, William G. *The Personal Life of David Livingstone*, London, John Murray, 1880

Boucher, M. (ed.) *Livingstone Letters 1843–1872: David Livingstone Correspondence in the Brenthurst Library*, Johannesburg, Brenthurst Press, 1985

Campbell, R.J. *Livingstone*, London, Ernest Benn, 1929

Chamberlin, D. (ed.) *Some Letters from Livingstone*, Oxford, Oxford University Press, 1940

Clendennen, G.W. *David Livingstone's Shire Journal 1861–1864*, Aberdeen, Scottish Cultural Press, 1992

Clendennen, G.W. and Cunningham, I.C. *David Livingstone: A Catalogue of Documents*, Edinburgh, National Library of Scotland, 1979

Coupland, Reginald *Livingstone's Last Journey*, London, Collins, 1945

Debenham, Frank *The Way to Ilala: David Livingstone's Pilgrimage*, London, 1955

De Lacerda, José *Reply to Dr Livingstone's Accusations and Misrepresentations*, London, Edward Stanford, 1865

Foskett, R. (ed.) *The Zambezi Doctors — David Livingstone's Letters to John Kirk 1858–1872*, Edinburgh, Edinburgh University Press, 1964

Fraser, Augusta Zelia *Livingstone and Newstead*, London, John Murray, 1913

Bibliography

Gelfand, Michael *Livingstone the Doctor: His Life and Travels*, Oxford, Blackwell, 1957

Healey, Edna *Wives of Fame*, London, Sidgwick and Jackson, 1986

Helly, Dorothy O. *Livingstone's Legacy: Horace Waller and Victorian Mythmaking*, Athens (Ohio), Ohio University Press, 1987

Holmes, Timothy *Journey to Livingstone: Exploration of an Imperial Myth*, Edinburgh, Canongate Press, 1993

——*David Livingstone, Letters and Documents 1841–1872: the Zambian Collection at the Livingstone Museum*, London and Bloomington, Currey, 1990

Huxley, Elspeth *Livingstone and his African Journey*, London, Weidenfeld, 1974

Jackson Haight, M.V. *European Powers and South-East Africa*, London, Routledge, 1967

Jeal, Tim *Livingstone*, London, Heinemann, 1973 (also Pimlico, 1993)

Johnston, H.H. *Livingstone and the Exploration of Central Africa*, London, George Philip & Sons, 1891

Livingstone, David *Missionary Travels and Researches in South Africa*, London, John Murray, 1857

Livingstone, D. and Livingstone, C. *Narrative of an Expedition to the Zambesi and its Tributaries; and the Discovery of Lakes Shirwa and Nyassa 1858–1864*, London, John Murray, 1865

Livingstone and Africa, proceedings of a seminar held on the occasion of the centenary of the death of David Livingstone, African Studies Centre, University of Edinburgh, 1973

Lloyd, B.W. (ed.) *Livingstone 1873–1973*, Cape Town, Struik, 1973

Macnair, J.I. *Livingstone the Liberator: A Study of a Dynamic Personality*, London, Collins, 1940

Martelli, George *Livingstone's River: A History of the Zambezi Expedition 1858–1864*, New York, Simon & Schuster, 1969

Monk, William (ed.) *Dr. Livingstone's Cambridge Lectures*, Cambridge, Deighton Bell & Co., 1858

National Portrait Gallery, *David Livingstone and the Victorian Encounter with Africa*, London, National Portrait Gallery Publications, 1996

Pachai, Bridglal (ed.) *Livingstone: Man of Africa. Memorial Essays 1873–1973*, London, Longman, 1973

Ransford, Oliver *David Livingstone: The Dark Interior*, London, John Murray, 1978

Schapera, Isaac (ed.) *David Livingstone: Family Letters 1841–1856*, 2 vols, London, Chatto & Windus, 1959

——*Livingstone's Private Journals 1851–1853*, London, Chatto & Windus, 1960

——*Livingstone's Missionary Correspondence 1841–1856*, London, Chatto & Windus, 1961

——*Livingstone's African Journal 1853–1856*, 2 vols, London, Chatto & Windus, 1963

——*David Livingstone: South African Papers 1849–1853*, Cape Town, Van Riebeeck Society, 2nd series, no. 5, 1974

Seaver, G. *David Livingstone: His Life and Letters*, London, Lutterworth, 1957

Shepperson, George (ed.) *David Livingstone and the Rovuma: A Notebook*, Edinburgh, Edinburgh University Press, 1965

Simmons, Jack *Livingstone and Africa*, London, English Universities Press, 1955

Simpson, Donald H. *Dark Companions: The African Contribution to the European Exploration of East Africa*, London, Paul Elek, 1975

Stanley, Henry M. *How I Found Livingstone*, London, Low, 1872

Tippu Tip *Maisha ya Hamed bin Muhammed el Murjebi yaani Tippu Tip*, Supplement to the East African Swahili Committee Journals, no. 28/2, July 1958, and no. 29/1, January 1959

Waller, Horace (ed.) *The Last Journals of David Livingstone in Central Africa from 1865 to his Death. Continued by a Narrative of his Last Moments and Sufferings, obtained from his faithful Servants Susi and Chuma*, London, John Murray, 1874

Wallis, J.P.R. (ed.) *The Zambezi Expedition of David Livingstone 1858–1863*, 2 vols, London, Chatto & Windus, 1956

——*The Zambezi Journal of James Stewart*, London, Chatto & Windus, 1952

Waters, John *David Livingstone, Trail Blazer*, Leicester, Inter-Varsity Press, 1996

POCKET BIOGRAPHIES

AVAILABLE

Beethoven
Anne Pimlott Baker

Scott of the Antarctic
Michael De-la-Noy

Alexander the Great
E.E. Rice

Sigmund Freud
Stephen Wilson

Marilyn Monroe
Sheridan Morley and
Ruth Leon

Rasputin
Harold Shukman

Jane Austen
Helen Lefroy

Mao Zedong
Delia Davin

Ellen Terry
Moira Shearer

Abraham Lincoln
H.G. Pitt

Charles Dickens
Catherine Peters

David Livingstone
C.S. Nicholls

FORTHCOMING

Marie and Pierre Curie
John Senior

Margot Fonteyn
Alastair Macaulay

Winston Churchill
Robert Blake

Enid Blyton
George Greenfield

FORTHCOMING

George IV
Michael De-la-Noy

Christopher Wren
James Chambers

W.G. Grace
Donald Trelford

Che Guevara
Andrew Sinclair

The Brontës
Kathryn White

Martin Luther King
Harry Harmer

Lawrence of Arabia
Jeremy Wilson

Christopher Columbus
Peter Riviere

For a copy of our complete list or details of other Sutton titles, please contact Regina Schinner at Sutton Publishing Limited, Phoenix Mill, Thrupp, Stroud, Gloucestershire, GL5 2BU